After the Lesson Plan

Realities of High School Teaching

After the Lesson Plan

Realities of High School Teaching

AMY PUETT EMMERS, Ph.D.

Ridgewood High School
Ridgewood, New Jersey

TEACHERS COLLEGE, COLUMBIA UNIVERSITY
NEW YORK AND LONDON 1981

Published by Teachers College Press, 1234 Amsterdam Avenue
New York, New York 10027

Library of Congress Cataloging in Publication Data

Emmers, Amy Puett, 1937–
  After the lesson plan.

  Includes index.
  1. High school teaching. 2. School discipline.
  3. Teacher-student relationships. I. Title.
  LB1607.E5   373.11'02   81-156
                                        AACR2
  ISBN 0-8077-2605-2 (paper)
  ISBN 0-8077-2654-0 (cloth)

Manufactured in the United States of America

  86   85   84   83   82   81   1   2   3   4   5   6

To the Memory of My Mother
And to My Aunt Co,
Both Teachers,
My First and Best Teachers

CONTENTS

FOREWORD

Some of the best-selling books in America today claim to induct their readers into the joys of cooking, the joys of fly casting, or the joys of some other activity. Many popular books and articles about teaching, on the other hand, eschew the whole notion of joy and focus on burn-out, incompetency, and ineffective schools, where students neither read nor write, let alone enjoy learning. *After the Lesson Plan* is a rare exception. While this book clearly deals with the realities of high school teaching, it does more than that; it shares with us the joy that Amy Emmers has found in being an exceptionally competent professional teacher. The book generates its own sense of excitement about teaching. Reading it makes us oldsters want to go quickly back into the high school classroom, not to avoid problems and realities, but to test our own wit, to see if we can be as clever a professional as Amy Emmers reveals herself to be. Prospective and new teachers are sure to find it equally exciting. Here they will discover a useful life raft when they find themselves in those early "sink or swim" years. The standards Dr. Emmers sets for professional survival, however, are very high.

For me, knowing Dr. Emmers' standards is not a discovery. It's more like a reassurance. Some fifteen years ago, before leaving for Teachers College, I worked with some Ridgewood High School teachers to initiate a program in American studies. Over the years that program has won plaudits from the school's most knowing critics—its students. We have always known that when excellence exists in the classroom, it is found in what teachers do day after day. Through this book, we can now share what Amy Emmers' students have learned in a special way: professional teaching can be a joy. And, for us, teaching can be a greater joy if we can learn to respond after the lesson plan.

Frank L. Smith, Jr.
Teachers College, Columbia University

ACKNOWLEDGMENTS

I am grateful to Ridgewood, New Jersey, Public Schools for the sabbatical year during which I wrote this manuscript. Several colleagues and friends aided me in its preparation, and for that I am also appreciative. Eileen Robinson and Tom LaValle, both of Ridgewood High School, made valuable suggestions for improving parts of the work, as did Wallace Douglas of Northwestern University and Paul Batty, formerly of Indiana University and now at Parkland College, Champaign, Illinois. Barry Qualls of Rutgers University coined the title and tirelessly helped me to edit the manuscript. In his own words, Qualls "cut with the precision of a surgeon." Since his operation was necessarily without anesthesia, it was sometimes painful, but it was always beneficial.

My husband Raimond was my first sounding board as I was writing. He often laughed that he could measure the worth of his comments by how hotly I rejected them—at first. For his endurance, his wisdom, and his encouragement, I am especially thankful.

INTRODUCTION

Students laughed wildly as I entered twenty minutes late through a door that did not want to yield to me. I took my place before them without the slightest idea of what I would say or do. I had no plan for that day's lesson, nor did I have any notion of what I would teach for the rest of that year. My stomach was queasy. Some of the laughter turned to sneers.

That's about all I remember now of a dream I had in early September some years ago. For a long time I never told anyone about this nightmare because I imagined that my fear of being unprepared was somehow shameful and abnormal. What I could not hide, though, was my laryngitis during the first week of school for the first three years I taught. I had majored in history at a well-known university, had taken the required number of education courses for certification in social studies, had practice-taught with a helpful master teacher, but I didn't feel at all prepared to face the tenth-graders before me and to teach them American government. Knowing that my uneasiness was not unique, that virtually all teachers experience it initially and have recurrent bouts of it, may not have solved my problems, but it would have made my heart lighter. Indeed, as I have since discovered, the pages of literature and history bristle with examples of beginners' agonies. Mr. Chips, beloved teacher of several generations of boys, presided over chaos during his first term. Henry Adams, regarded by many as a brilliant historian, felt unprepared to teach that subject when he commenced his duties at Harvard.

This book is intended, then, for those like myself and many others who doubt initially their ability to teach or who encounter sufficient trials to make them seriously question their competence. It assumes that while great teaching is an individual matter, there is still much about the mastery of the profession that can be passed on to those truly interested in careers in secondary teaching. Remembering the various pitfalls that almost ensnared me, I hope that others will be amused and helped by the anecdotes gathered from schools in which I have worked or from friends at other schools. If my ideas appear at last to be more common sense than sophisticated pedagogy, I have found that common sense is often uncommonly long in surfacing to our consciousness.

Frequently people ask how anyone today could possibly want to teach. The critics of modern youth claim that they are disrespectful of authority, as well as unappreciative of what schools do for them. That may be, but what those critics fail to consider is how students themselves see school. Even teachers often lose sight of the students' perspective. That is natural enough since classes have to be a major part of every teacher's life, while any given class is relatively insignificant to students. Chapter I recalls the students' point of view: What do they think a good class is? What do they expect of teachers? Let a new teacher not be duped into believing that he knows these answers merely because he himself has recently been a student. For some reason this knowledge mysteriously vanishes as soon as he switches roles.

Beginning and experienced teachers alike may find it reassuring to know that regardless of current fads the basic precepts of good teaching are fairly simple and they don't change much over the years. First, a teacher must gain his students' attention. So elementary an idea may seem to require no fanfare, but maintaining the attention of captive listeners is not easy unless they are motivated to learn. Various techniques for gaining students' attention and fostering their motivation are suggested in Chapter II. Second, although a teacher should never ask students to do anything they can't, he must insist that they perform at the level of their ability. To do this well, a teacher must be able to recognize degrees of ability and to distinguish incapable students from lazy or unmotivated ones (Chapter III). These two principles of instruction are endorsed by almost all educators. However, the principles are ineffective without a third: learning must be rewarded, failure to learn penalized. For some reason this third principle has become unpopular today. Many educators believe that rewards and punishments are inappropriate in classrooms unless the reward is one of accomplishment itself and punishment the self-inflicted one of not learning. As attractive as that argument may be, it disregards human nature since it implies that people are more self-sufficient than they seem to be. Chapter II analyzes the controversy and, together with Chapter III, offers a number of rewards and penalties teachers may find helpful.

These three principles are so basic to instruction that they apply to almost any kind of learning. One can use them to teach a dog to obey, to teach a child to walk and speak, and to teach high school students their history, mathematics, English, or whatever. Of course, the specific applications of the principles differ in these instances. The principles do not vary because our measure of knowing something does not vary. Learning has occurred when a task is performed on command: that applies to a dog's shaking hands, a child's walking across the room, or a high school student's solving a physics problem. While it may be that an individual can know how to solve a problem without being willing to show that to others, his ability remains debatable. By this definition, a thoughtful beginning teacher may recognize that reading these principles will not imply that he has learned them. Even if he can recite them, he will not yet be able to apply them to his subject. At least, though, he knows what he has to learn, something often obscured by various theories of education.

Ironically, a beginner doesn't have to know a great deal about his subject to be successful in the classroom. Beginners are often incorrectly advised that success is almost guaranteed if they know their subjects thoroughly. Nothing could be further from the truth, nothing more impossible. At whatever level in whatever field, if a teacher knows his subject at all he knows how little about that field he actually knows. Moreover, neither students nor adults measure success in teaching solely by knowledge of subject. The most erudite persons on a faculty will be scorned if all they know are details of their subject.

A beginner will thus be given a chance on the job to learn not only what to teach but also how to teach. After a month or two in the classroom, he may think that the hardest thing he has to learn is how to maintain order. Most teachers who "cry before Christmas"—and many do—cry over discipline problems. But how can a teacher recognize the difference between mischief and more serious forms of misbehavior? What makes one class cooperative and another unruly, even when the teacher and the subject remain the same? How strict should teachers be? Questions like these are at the heart of Chapter IV.

In the difficult days of the first year when a teacher can barely stay one day ahead of students, let alone one week, he should remember that students come and go quickly in a school, while its staff remains fairly constant. What this means really, even though it is seldom acknowledged, is that classroom success is less important initially in keeping a job than friendly cooperation with other adults in the building. Chapter V suggests how administrators, older teachers, specialists, and nonprofessional workers see their work and the behavior they appreciate from first-year teachers.

The thorniest topic of all, the goals of education, is reserved for Chapter VI. Implicit throughout those pages is the question, What is good teaching? As difficult as the term may be to explain in words, all of us can identify good teachers. A good teacher doesn't have to "love his kids," in the sense in which that phrase is commonly meant. Loving has nothing to do with instruction. A good teacher may be gently persuasive, harshly autocratic, or anywhere between these extremes. However. all good

teachers have one characteristic in common: they wish to help students learn, not simply to excel as teachers. In focusing his attention on students, a good teacher not only assists them in mastering a particular skill, but also interprets for them some truth about what it means to be human. Most importantly, a good teacher must himself understand that education includes more than book learning, and he must help students acquire this broader kind of education.

Reading about the reality of life in a secondary school should make a beginner's plight, if not less demanding, at least easier to accept and understand. The rewards can be many, as explored briefly in the epilogue (Chapter VII). Among those is knowing that education is, in Henry Adams' words, a "serious thing." Adams even resigned his position at Harvard because he felt unable to fulfill the high duties of the office. However, the responsibility Adams describes need not be overwhelming, and it can become the inspiration for any teacher's career:

A parent gives life, but as parent gives no more. A murderer takes life, but his deed stops there. A teacher affects eternity; he can never tell where his influence stops.[*]

---

[*]*The Education of Henry Adams: An Autobiography* (Boston: Houghton Mifflin, 1961), p. 300.

I

Students' View of School

If parents and educators could climb inside their youngsters' minds and see school as they do, the sight would probably startle them! That shock would be one of recognition though. Everyone has been a student, everyone knows how a student feels, but as quickly as a person assumes adulthood, he tends to forget. Different "eyes" give an altered perspective.

When Johnnies and Janes across America set out for high school each morning, their parents may well sigh with relief that for a few hours someone else will be responsible for their children's nurture and safety. The sons and daughters, however, already think they are responsible for themselves in most situations, and they certainly won't admit that they need anyone to care for them. Unlike teachers and school officials, students don't have to be particularly concerned that their school operates effectively and efficiently. They set out each day to have as pleasant a time as possible in a place where they must spend most of their days for most of each year and where most of their time is planned for them. What do they see as the purpose of their classes and extracurricular activities? What do they expect from school employees? How do they regard the physical environment of a school, includ-

1

ing materials and equipment? Recalling the students' point of view, especially as it pertains to classroom teachers, may at times be unsettling, but it should also at times be amusing and helpful.

Purpose of School: Social and Academic

Near graduation several years ago, a senior whom I had taught appraised his high school experience for me. While he acknowledged that he had not been as good a student as he might have been—his grade average was C—he had few regrets about high school. He believed that he had plenty of time in college to make up any academic deficiencies. What he was especially proud of was his standing among his friends. They had elected him king of homecoming and best-all-around from the boys in the senior class. In his own words, "High school has been good to me."

Most high school students would agree with him. Of course, if a student is asked explicitly why he goes to high school, he will almost always say he goes to be educated. However, when he himself thinks of school, he as often recalls his friends as he does his courses. Learning American history pales in comparison to hearing about a previous night's party; solving algebraic equations intrigues less than figuring out how to be acceptable before one's peers. Rarely will academic advancement be more vital to a student than his social development; rarely will studying consume more of his energy than socializing. Their view of schooling is as natural as it is realistic. Any given class or a combination of them all is likely to be a relatively insignificant part of a student's total life, while his very self-image in part reflects how his friends regard him. Students see that their elders, except perhaps a small percentage of professionals, derive more pleasure from their relationships with other people than from their work. Moreover, many students realize that society rewards a person for important social contacts more than for knowledge.

While instant and future benefits of social development are apparent, many students get no immediate reward from academic work at all. A student may have little or no inclination or ability to study, say, world literature or biology. He may see little prac-

cause that night the snowstorm we all frequently prayed for came. She laughed, of course, but I think to a certain extent she still resented the fact that she had unnecessarily missed that game. There was no question that we preferred having fun with each other to work.

Furthermore, we may confuse students today by telling them that learning is "fun." That semantic juggling is little more than a sleight-of-hand. What educators mean is that once a person can perform a task, he will usually derive pleasure from doing it. If it is a difficult task, he also has the specialist's pleasure of knowing that he can do something many others can't. The actual learning, though, is work. Playing a Chopin waltz accurately and artistically will give any pianist pleasure. To get to the point where he can do this, he must struggle many hours, literally perfecting the piece measure by measure. Is that fun?

The work of a course is usually not the first thing students have in mind when they say they have had a good class. A good class is one in which they feel at ease both with the teacher and with each other; because they don't have to be overly concerned about what others are thinking of them, they can act naturally and spontaneously. That doesn't mean they're free to do or say anything, but they're reasonably sure of what's permissible. They know their teacher won't hesitate to digress from the lesson if they have something else as important or interesting on their minds. (Incidentally, sometimes digressions can be the best part of a class for the teacher as well as for students.)

Students also expect to be amused some of the time in a good class. They are used to a high level of professional entertainment on TV. How can any teacher match that? In addition, the routine of a class and of the school day frequently bores students. To relieve the monotony, resourceful students in all grades invent games. As an example, after one of my senior classes the other year, I discovered a sort of marathon note, which had been passed from student to student. All of them had tried to write something funny about our discussion of *Long Day's Journey into Night;* apparently they had a contest of sorts to see who could top the previous one-liner.

Games like that don't really disrupt a class. They are not intended to insult a teacher or criticize his skill of presentation. Since they are harmless, the best solution is to ignore them. Trying to incorporate games into lessons will not stop students from inventing their own games. They understand the difference between a game they think up for mere fun and a teacher's "game," which ends in the students having to know something. A pill is still a pill, for all its sugar-coating. Students want—often demand—some classroom fun that isn't lesson-oriented. Moreover, if a teacher is so strict that he never allows any kind of diversion from the lesson, he creates a situation ripe for another time-tested game, "Get the Teacher." It is hilarious to students, even though they won't necessarily laugh out loud, if they can harass a teacher with a trifling annoyance, such as hiding erasers before a class begins.

Their insistence on entertainment notwithstanding, a good class is one in which students are required to learn some facts or concepts or skills they have not known before. Without this condition students feel they are wasting their time in a class, something they dislike almost as much as never having any fun. Students know, though, that there is more to life than amassing facts, and most students realize they will soon forget many of the facts and skills teachers require them to learn. Students resent having to memorize the names and symbols of chemical elements, the names and dates of various presidential administrations, the four major uses of the comma, unless they get at least an inkling of why they should. Therefore, a good class is one in which the teacher knows and reveals the rationale for learning the various details of the subject.

If youngsters grant that book learning is an essential part of school, they don't think it should always take priority over other activities. Most students would probably like to be involved in extracurricular activities, even though not all of them are. The rewards of a football field, a concert hall, or a stage are many and more tangible than an A on an examination could ever be. Students may bask in the adulation of their school, their family, and even their town. Prizes and scholarships may also be at stake. Aside from the glory, the activities are valuable and sometimes blossom into careers. Even selling tickets or stuffing envelopes can be rewarding if a student feels that makes him part of a group.

Like almost everybody else, teachers favor student participation in extracurricular activities, but teachers also fear that those activities may consume too much student energy. Often that does happen. A neighbor remarked recently that to her son football was school; classes he could take or leave. Teachers believe they must oppose this view; extracurricular activities are fine as long as they don't interfere with academic progress. When that happens there is likely to be conflict among students, teachers, and even administrators. Students, for instance, are usually happy when their extracurricular activities allow them to skip a class. Their attitude is that they can't possibly miss much in one or several sessions. They may have to wrangle with a teacher about the absence, especially when the activity is unrelated to a teacher's own discipline. Science teachers dislike having students miss a science class to rehearse for a concert; English teachers fume about early dismissals for math meets or athletic events. Teachers don't know whether to be more irritated with students for participating in an organization or with administrators for providing the official sanction for the absence. Besides impeding students' progress, those absences create more work for teachers.

That stance is nit-picking to students. Most don't realize that teachers may be genuinely inconvenienced by absences. If a student misses a test, he thinks a teacher can pull another one from a file for him or at most spend only several minutes composing another. Moreover, even those students who better understand the work of teachers expect them to be willing to sacrifice for activities that enhance not only an individual student's life but also the life of the entire school community. Teachers should agree.

Characteristics of the "Average" Student

A usual or general student has been mentioned numerous times in these pages. Undoubtedly readers are remembering students who don't think or act at all like the ones described here. To be sure, some students simply refuse to work or to participate in school life; others care more about their studies and school than some of their teachers. Some students are retarded; others are extremely gifted intellectually. However, for every one of these exceptional students, many others belong somewhere between the extremes. Because it is with this majority of students that most teachers must work for most of their careers, it is valuable to master the general case before concerning oneself with exceptions. Moreover, learning to teach students with these usual attitudes and behavior is often more difficult than learning to cope with exceptions. The majority are interested in becoming educated. They merely lack an intense desire to learn, and that's what teachers have to try to help them achieve.

These so-called average students vary somewhat, depending upon their grade level in high school. Freshmen and sophomores, recent graduates of junior high or middle school, are concerned with numerous extra-academic matters. (Those grades are considered as one here since in many communities high school does not begin until the sophomore year.) Temporarily their promotion to the "big" school is a demotion as well. No longer able to star, lead, and lord it over younger students, most freshmen and sophomores are a little frightened as they try to understand as quickly as possible the ways of high school. Underclassmen must become accustomed to new buildings, new teachers, new schedules, and new school rules. They must also learn what is acceptable conduct before their peers, an ever fresh and engaging subject to them. What are they supposed to wear to school? How long should their hair be? Are they supposed to be friendly with everyone in the halls or just with certain people? Is it all right to go to a party alone, or should they always be with others? Less sophisticated than they are often assumed to be, these boys and girls are quite unsure about their emotional relationship to each other. They may have sexual experiences at an earlier age than used to be the case, but that doesn't imply that they are confident about how they should act around the opposite sex. If they are left to choose their own seats in a room, almost inevitably a "boys' side" and a "girls' side" will emerge. It is something of an event when and if mixed couples appear.

Their uncertainty about all of these things, as well as their youth, makes freshmen and sophomores the silliest and most disorderly students in high school. Often at the least provocation, ninth- and tenth-graders are consumed with giggles. Boys especially still like to throw spitballs and erasers and paper airplanes. They test authority frequently as they attempt to prove themselves the toughest kids in school. Clearly academic work could never be as pressing to underclassmen as their other personal concerns.

Eleventh-graders are the most teachable of high school levels. They have learned what they can and what they cannot get by with, and age alone makes them more cooperative than younger students. The most momentous event in the lives of almost all juniors is becoming a licensed driver: that sheet of paper certifying that they can move independently not only means hours of pleasure for them but also indicates society's recognition of their coming-of-age. Another indicator of that is the Social Security number many of them are issued as they become employed for the first time. If juniors are also college preparatory students, they are usually more dedicated to their studies than they were previously. Their motivation derives partly from their facing both the preliminary and final versions of the Scholastic Aptitude Tests (SAT's) and partly from their knowing that the transcript of the junior year's record is especially important to college admissions officers. Even most eleventh-graders who are not college-bound, however, still seem to regard high school as an acceptable way of life. They are not yet close enough to graduation to fret about a totally different life-style.

Such acquiescence does not apply to a great number of seniors, although exactly what happens to them over the summer is somewhat unclear. Perhaps as they grow older, they yearn more for independence. Perhaps they are affected by the nearness of their goal. They may simply be tired of school: twelve years is a long time from the perspective of a seventeen-year-old. In any event, from the beginning of their twelfth grade, many really want to be out of high school. They feel they are marking time, often to no end other than their diplomas. College preparatory seniors, on the other hand, continue to take their schoolwork seriously in the beginning of the year. They want the transcript of the first half of their senior year, the part that colleges scrutinize, to be as good as they can make it. Virtually all seniors, though, hit "senior slump." Likely to start any time between January and June, this marks the end of much schoolwork for them. They do what they feel they must, but high school is in reality, if not in fact, over for them.

Although their attitude can make teaching seniors harrowing, they're personally the most sophisticated of the levels. Unlike underclassmen, they will more likely express their lack of interest by sitting quietly or by absenting themselves rather than by disturbing a class. By the time they graduate, most of them will be legally adults; they are beginning to assume more responsibility for themselves. Some of them have paying jobs. Many have serious boyfriends or girlfriends. Rare seniors are even married and have children of their own. I like to tease my twelfth-graders by telling them that by the time they are seniors they are almost human.

Students' Conception of School Employees

When students generalize about school personnel, they usually have teachers in mind. Most students have only a vague notion of what administrators, for instance, do, since those officers are available to them for only a limited time. In schools with large populations students may not even know what the chief administrator looks like. It amuses me to hear students confuse administrative and teacher responsibility, assuming in their innocence that teachers have more power than they do. If a teacher needs some piece of equipment, students wonder why he doesn't order it. If something is wrong with a school's schedule, they wonder why teachers don't change it. However, one administrative function about which all students are clear is the disciplinary one. If they misbehave badly enough, they will be sent to a dean or principal. Because of this authority, students are awed by administrators.

Except for hesitation they may feel in the presence of any adult, students are seldom awed by other workers in a school. Students understand that it is the duty of noninstructional personnel to aid them. That attitude presents little difficulty to a guidance counselor, a psychologist, a nurse, and any others who generally help students on a one-to-one basis. A librarian, though, may be exasperated in trying to enforce his policies unless he has strong administrative support. Students realize that a librarian per se has little effective authority over them. The same applies to paraprofessional and nonprofessional workers. If a janitor wants students to help clean an area they have soiled, he must have a great deal of friendly persuasion, personal clout, or the strong threat of administrative intervention to get them to do it. Students expect workers in a school to serve them and not to bother them.

Because they must work for their teachers, students usually do not perceive that teachers too serve them. How could they be expected to know that a teacher works for them as much as if not more than they do for him? Because of this and because a teacher has the power of the grade, most students don't understand that they can and do demand very much of a teacher. They are much more likely to be concerned about what he demands of them. There is a catch, though, to what is probably sounding like an ideal situation. Since students respect the authority of a teacher's position, even though they may or may not respect him as an individual, they expect from a teacher the behavior and attitudes that usually accompany positions of authority. Deny it as vehemently as they often will, students want to look up to a teacher. A teacher may occasionally like to keep students guessing by foiling their anticipations, but he may also put himself at a disadvantage if he shocks them unintentionally. He needs to understand what students regard as "proper" teacher behavior. (Incidentally, these ideas apply generally to all professionals in a school even though they are directed particularly to teachers.)

One of the first things students notice about any teacher is his appearance. I was befuddled when a boy in one of my classes announced that my students never expected me to be available to them after hours on Thursdays. They knew, he explained, that Thursday was my "hair" day. At first I wondered how that rascal had learned so much about my personal habits, but the answer wasn't far off. Each Wednesday and Thursday they saw me become increasingly in need of a shampoo. Then on Friday, *voilà!* a new coiffure. Because a teacher is constantly on display, students can't help being aware of the way he looks. Moreover, appearance is extremely important to teen-agers. Always anxious about how they look to others, many of them groom themselves for hours. Even the unkempt look among adolescents is often a studied one.

Every faculty has members who are always chicly attired, as well as others who inevitably appear mismatched no matter what they wear. Some teachers never seem to wear the same outfit twice; others always appear to have on the same thing. Still others apparently have particular attire assigned to every day of the week, and they never confuse Wednesday's costume with Tuesday's. Even though clothes may not make a person, they do reflect who he is or whom he hopes to be. Students laugh at attire that is conspicuous for whatever reason. For example, it is funny to them that a man wears narrow ties when wide ones are in vogue. However, they also joke about teachers who are extremely fashion-conscious. One article in a student newspaper described a "leisure suited" dean who upon promotion to principal became a "double-breasted" conservative. What is not at all acceptable is for teachers to try to ape students' dress; that spoils a generation's attempt to be unique.

A discussion of clothing in a book for professionals may seem offensive, but apparently there are misconceptions about appropriate classroom attire. On the one hand, many people associate "good" teachers with schoolmarms or masters in neat blue or gray. Ironically, even the most modish on a staff sometimes think that conservative attire is the most appropriate for teachers, or at least they believe that others find it so. On the other hand, some imagine that teachers can wear absolutely anything they want in the classroom. Although dress today is as flexible for teachers as it is for students, the carte blanche approach ignores the obvious. Most people wouldn't wear the same clothes to a funeral that they would to a cocktail party; they wouldn't go dancing in their tennis togs. A reliable guide for teachers is the clothing an adult would wear to a white-collar business or professional office. Because administrators expect teachers to conform to this general standard, flagrant disregard of it may have a negative influence on hiring and promotion.

As evident as a teacher's appearance is his speech. To speak anything other than standard English is to open oneself to ridicule or worse, since even unsophisticated students usually recognize some of the discrepancies between standard and nonstandard language. An extreme instance occurred in a southern community, one in which most of the students' own speech contained any number of nonstandard forms, including hobgoblins like "I ain't got none." Nevertheless, one new teacher was mocked by pupils for saying, "Git yer lags frum 'round them cheer rims and set up straight." They may have been laughing primarily at his dialect, which differed markedly from theirs, but many also recognized his grammatical errors. Students don't think it's all right for a teacher to do something merely because they themselves do it.

While students usually do not object to a teacher's using slang or hip talk, those forms change so rapidly that by the time a teacher uses an expression, it will already sound a little antiquated to students. A few years ago "tough" was the word adolescents used to express approval of something, but by the time I became aware of their coinage, it had already been replaced. If I use "groovy" or "neat," my generation's slang for approval, my students will indulge me but not without smiling because they find these words rather peculiar ways to express approval as, ironically, my elders also did. One reason for the short life of much slang is that each generation insists on new vocabulary as a way of differentiating itself from previous groups; for that reason alone students probably prefer to keep their expressions for themselves. As soon as these inventions are adopted by the general populace, the expressions will be changed anyway.

Students are less tolerant about faculty use of profanity or vulgarities. Alert ears in the halls of any American high school will detect many four-letter words studded throughout students' casual conversations with each other. Notwithstanding, most students will not use such language around teachers unless the students are provoked. If they slip before a teacher and utter even a mild obscenity, they are usually embarrassed and their classmates are embarrassed for them. Their knowing and using the words themselves doesn't mean they are pleased by hearing them regularly from a teacher. Sometimes as a year progresses I feel comfortable enough with a group to let out a spontaneous "hell" or "damn." Students laugh at this if the situation has obviously frustrated or angered me; they say it means I am "human." If I used swear words commonly, though, as I did when I first began teaching, students might wonder what I was trying to prove.

The most misunderstood student expectation of teachers is the students' frequently voiced stipulation that they want their teachers to be their friends. At the beginning of one year, a tenth-grader asked her French teacher if she could call her by her first name. The student added that in junior high their teachers had allowed that because those teachers had been their friends. Instead of replying yes or no, the French teacher asked this student if she would like to go to dinner or to the movies with her. The student was totally nonplused.

Her teacher then explained to her that although she hoped they would remain friendly, they could not truly be friends. The equilibrium necessary to friendship is prohibited to students and teachers by the very nature of their relationship. Most friendship arises out of similar tastes and interests. Even when a person is a twenty-two-year-old teacher working with eighteen-year-old students, age alone effectively prevents friendship. Nobody who is twenty-two really wants to go to a high school dance or pep rally, any more than a high school student wants to attend those functions at a junior high. More importantly, true friendship necessitates willingness to sacrifice for the befriended. Should students be put in a position to have to sacrifice for a teacher? Students often say that if a certain teacher is their friend, they can go to that teacher with their problems. Who, however, would not look askance at a teacher who regularly went to students with his troubles? Friendship means that kind of give-and-take. When a student approaches a teacher with his problems, he is not approaching him as a friend with whom he hopes to reciprocate, but as an adviser.

Students like teachers who are amiable, considerate, and optimistic. Students also want their teachers to be willing to help them—and in more ways than with their studies. Above all, they want teachers to be fair, fair about classroom deportment and fair about grades. A teacher who plays favorites will not be a favorite with any student for long, not even with the favored. In short, students simply want to be able to revere their teachers; it's easier to work for and learn from those we respect.

Students' Perspective of a School's Physical Environment

Most American high schools today are better equipped than they have ever been before. Why, then, parents and teachers query, aren't students more appreciative of these facilities? Materials are often wantonly abused, and even in our so-called best communities vandalism and theft are commonplace. What parents and teachers frequently fail to do, though, is to see the physical plant and materials from the students' standpoint.

The overall tone or atmosphere of a school influences the way students feel about its facilities. Most high schools are closed campuses, since administrators, teachers, parents, and community businessmen consider this the most efficient way to operate a school. A closed campus means that students are restricted to a building or buildings and grounds for approximately seven hours a day. Certain parts of buildings, including hallways, are off-limits to students for the greater part of a day. If they do have permission to be in corridors while classes are in session, frequently they are not allowed to talk there because teachers don't like to compete with their noise. Within a classroom students are almost always limited to the same seat for each period and usually they must retain it for an entire year. From those seats they must deliver answers to all sorts of questions unless they want to be embarrassed or penalized or both. Moreover, many schools stipulate that when students are not in classes, they must be in other designated rooms, thereby restricting their unsupervised time to those approximately five-minute intervals between classes. More and more schools are even finding it necessary to employ security guards to enforce order. These conditions, endorsed by most educators, parents, and communities at large, may help to make a school operate smoothly, but they also share much in common with another institution in our society: the prison.

Naturally enough, students often complain that their schools are jails, their teachers guards. No self-respecting high school students think they need supervision in their free time at school any more than they think they need it in their free time after school. They wonder why, for example, they can't go to a store at ten o'clock as well as at four, provided they don't have classes. Why should older people think students will invariably get into mischief or more serious trouble if they manage their own time? Perhaps they would prefer to do their homework at night when they cannot visit with their friends. Perhaps, as their elders fear, they would prefer not to study. Students wonder what happened to their right of choice. If they protest that they're being treated like babies or prisoners, teachers are apt to laugh and say that they don't know what they're talking about or that they don't know what's good for them. Nevertheless, students feel abused, and this feeling may find an outlet in rebellious, sometimes destructive behavior. The destruction may be a way of letting off steam as much as retaliation against specific wrongs.

The design of a school plant also contributes to its atmosphere and to the way students regard the school. In any era the design of schools, like that of other public buildings, reflects current architectural trends. Many schools built in the 1920s, for instance, imitate the imposing columns of classical temples, while those constructed after World War II frequently look like overgrown ranch houses or motels. This predictability of style is coupled

with another equally predictable condition: practicality rather than aesthetics dictates school plans. The unappealing architectural structures that for the most part result employ virtually no unique design at all. Often they are a hodgepodge of several styles.

Furthermore, after the elementary level, schools are not decorated with students' tastes in mind. While it is true that some high schools are replacing institutional green walls with multicolored ones, this indicates a fashion in interior design more than it does students' desires. Actually, adults might not like what students chose if they were free to decorate schools; sections of stores and other public areas designed to attract adolescents usually don't appeal to persons over thirty. I remember being horrified by a class's surprise for its teacher when we resumed school after Christmas one year. A hideously bright yellow wall boasted a starkly black silhouette of Clint Eastwood three times larger than life. Teaching with that giant scrutinizing my every move would have been nearly impossible for me.

However, if students could select their school's interior design, the rooms might at least be decorated. Except for an occasional back-to-school night when we spruce up for parents, most high school halls and rooms are desolate. Halls are usually windowless and lined on either side with metal lockers looking like so many erect soldiers. If a building is over thirty years old, pipes in both its halls and rooms are almost invariably exposed. Classrooms may appear cluttered even when they are neat, since they must accommodate great numbers of desks. In fact, being in a classroom is somewhat like being in a furniture showroom of unattractive and uncomfortable individual pieces, all of them exactly alike. Often in an entire school there are no comfortable places in which students may sit. Even lounges are usually appointed with hard metal and/or plastic chairs. While these may be durable, they are anything but attractive and inviting.

Other standard appointments in classrooms include chalkboards, an American flag, roll-down maps, and shades or blinds that are almost always ripped or broken or both. Sometimes rooms exhibit an appropriate but predictable picture or two. History rooms favor black-and-white glossies of imposing American leaders such as Washington or Jefferson or Kennedy; English ones may have writers like Shakespeare or Hawthorne staring down at students; and biology rooms sport Darwin or leaves and insects. Apparently to reassure or inspire students, an occasional motto is displayed: "Today is the first day of the rest of your life" is a favorite.

When it comes to blame for such ugliness, everyone likes to point in the other direction. Parents and administrators cry budgets. Teachers often feel helpless to change the bleakness. They are sometimes assigned to three or four different rooms, and while they are responsible for all of these generally, they are responsible for none particularly. Even if they teach in the same place all day, they may lack materials, time, or interest to decorate it. Most feel it would be educationally unfeasible to use student time to decorate rooms. Students say they would like a more pleasing environment, but they hesitate to work to produce it if they must do so after school. That is their time and they usually aren't generous about donating it.

Although schools must then appear to students as repressive, unattractive places, they don't focus on this dreariness as much as might be expected because they are occupied with their social lives and with the work and entertainment of a school. But should it surprise us really that they take so little pride in their schools? The problem is compounded by the question of ownership. Youngsters can be reminded that it's tax money—ultimately their money—that pays for facilities, but they don't feel this. They don't pay taxes yet, and except for hearing parents and teachers grumble in the middle of each April, the concept is meaningless for them.

The greatest part of student misuse and abuse of school facilities results from thoughtlessness. Litter, for instance, is a blemish on virtually every school. Classroom floors are usually well dotted with papers by the end of a day unless a teacher insists that the trash be picked up. If the desks have solid bottoms, they will quickly be crammed with papers, books, food, mittens, caps, anything that can be stuffed into them. Corridors and grounds are likewise strewn with all manner of trash. Areas designated or taken over for smoking are defaced with hundreds of butts. In defense of students, though, the problem is not exclusive to schools; any American public place quickly becomes littered if it does not employ an efficient janitorial service.

Enormous attrition of textbooks and other materials, equipment, and property is also hastened by thoughtlessness. The halls in one school had been recently painted. As students congregated in the main hall to wait for buses, they leaned against the wall, comfortably propping one foot against it as well. The students did not notice what they were doing; they had no intention of spoiling the wall; they were merely relaxing as they waited to leave the building. Nevertheless, within a week the main hall was so scuffed that it needed repainting.

Mischief also accounts for some of the abuse of school property. Without thinking of right or wrong, students simply want to have some fun. This is what they are doing when they leave their graffiti throughout a school. It often seems they like to write on everything but paper: desks, walls, equipment, nothing escapes their scribbles and carvings. By the way, a teacher can gauge students' feelings about himself and one another by those anonymous messages left on desks.

Cafeterias, notoriously undersized, are also frequent scenes of pranks. Students must wait in long lines for what are frequently unappetizing lunches. Mischief as often results from their having too little time to eat as it does from their having too much time left over. Even though teachers are usually assigned to watch over cafeteria sessions, students can zing a peanut past a teacher's head while his back is turned. Or they can plop a large blob of Jell-O in someone else's chair so that he will have a "cushion" when he returns to sit down. That may well signal the heavy artillery: oranges, apples, milk cartons, bread, even spaghetti and meat balls become missiles to hurl at adversaries. To a student, this is all in the name of fun. He doesn't consider the mess to clean up unless he is apprehended and made to do it himself, nor does he fret about a few broken dishes. Although administrators and teachers try to discourage and prohibit disorderliness, most also see this behavior as mischief unless someone gets hurt.

The line between mischief and vandalism, though, is sometimes a fine one, and what starts as mischief may become vandalism. One winter some students thought it would be very funny to roll a giant snowball down one of the corridors of their school. They worked and worked to shape a ball about five feet in diameter. So far, their plan was innocent enough; at the worst, classes would be disrupted for a little while. The situation changed drastically when they discovered a locked door to the corridor they intended to enter. Deciding to force the door open, they found it didn't give very easily. After they had hacked their way through it, the door had to be completely replaced, and their mischief had become a misdemeanor.

Nor are schools exempt from the out-and-out vandalism that has become increasingly rampant in our society. More and more schools must allot a larger and larger portion of their budgets to cover the destruction. Why are windows and lights broken? Why is paint thrashed on walls and doors? The motivation for the abuse is as mystifying to most students as it is to adults.

Psychologists distinguish the causes of vandalism from those of theft, which usually results from personal need or greed. School vandalism, they tell us, is the students' way of getting even. Destruction protests the fact that students feel neglected; they do not think that individually they matter very much to the school. This theory does explain some vandalism. However, it does not account for persons who enjoy destruction for its own sake. Certainly a child likes to tear down. Isn't he gleeful as he knocks over his own or his friend's castle of blocks? Some residue of this trait remains in most adults. We are drawn to fires and wrecks. We are attracted as quickly by a crane's demolition of one building as we are by a carpenter's construction of another. As Graham Greene's story "The Destructors" shows, tearing down can be as exciting as creating, demolition an inverted form of creation. Moreover, since our society is one with few taboos and with little effective punishment for violating even those taboos, a person may indulge a whim to destroy with little fear of retribution.

By talking with students over the years, I've come to believe that the way they see school can explain quite a bit about the way they act there. In some schools their view may be less dreary than the one suggested here; in others it may be worse. Whatever their conception, though, teachers should try to grasp it, for without that knowledge, they really cannot be very good teachers. They won't know when to teach and when to discipline.

A natural way for teachers to discover students' opinions is to take a few minutes of class time to let them talk about how they stand on a current issue in the school. Suppose a prohibition against smoking is pending. How do students feel about that? One warning: should a teacher invite this kind of discussion only to counter whatever students say with his own view, they are going to wonder why he asked for their opinions in the first place. On the other hand, students invariably enjoy these discussions if they feel their teacher is genuinely interested in their point of view. It is not that a teacher needs to agree with students, but he should not convey that he thinks they are foolish for thinking as they do. When students hear a teacher say something even as noncommittal as, "Oh, is that the way you think" or "I see what you mean," then they know that teacher cares about their feelings. That attitude encourages confidence in the teacher and willingness to cooperate.

If students regard the regimentation of schools as repressive—as I believe most do to some degree—should and can teachers do anything to change that? To answer, we must seek the causes of that feeling. Many students, for example, dislike having to work according to a schedule. As we'll see in a later chapter, though, teachers know that the schedule cannot be disregarded without loss to students.

However, the cause of students' disaffection also lies with society's demands of its schools. While nobody thinks schools should be prisons, schools are expected to be more than learning centers.

They are also supposed to keep students out of trouble and off the streets. This implies that students can't be trusted to manage much of their free time, even eighteen-year-old seniors who are legally adults. The truth is that although unlimited freedom for students would be as undesirable as total confinement, most of them need to be free to do more than study. That is heavy fare even for professional scholars. How useful can students feel if all they're supposed to do all day, every day is study or play? They don't want to be baby-sat or to postpone living. Most of them would like to be and probably should be more personally and financially responsible than they are. Many teachers who recognize the legitimacy of these concerns nevertheless feel powerless to do much about them.

A final question, then, remains: how can a teacher in good conscience enforce rules that he thinks are not altogether in students' best interests? How, for instance, can he try to require them to work silently in a study hall if he thinks they might be better off elsewhere? The answer is simple. He does it because it's a part of his job. Teachers do not establish school policy; rather they carry out what their administrators, together with the Board of Education, decide will be best for the community. Few teachers have time, energy, or talent to be social innovators. Their efforts are centered in the classroom.

And it is in the classroom that teachers hold a trump card. If classrooms are lively, students can become oblivious to other complaints. Moreover, even given the most ideal environment, youngsters will never like school very much unless they find that academic work is interesting or that it is related to the problems of living. Helping them want to learn in these ways is probably the greatest contribution teachers can make to their lives.

II
Helping Students Want to Learn

In the so-called golden days of education, old-timers like to remind us, polite students came to school motivated to learn. There was no nonsense either; all cooperated for good schools. The trouble with kids today is they don't want to learn. If these critics of today's generation seem somewhat hazy about the actual days of yore, they do understand the process of learning. They realize that unless students are motivated to learn, neither they nor their teachers will achieve very much.

High school and college teachers today may feel that they are faced with more and more youngsters with no other incentive for learning than society's "requirement" for higher and higher levels of education. However, modern students are most likely no less motivated than students in the past. This generation is simply less afraid to make known what they don't like. Any student, even one generally motivated toward academic success, will be unenthusiastic about learning the subject matter of a given course unless he is first shown why he should. For teachers to devote time and energy to this is not catering to students' lack of purpose: the first principle of learning has always been that before anyone can be taught something, he must first be attracted to the task. Beginning with the first day of school—one of the most important of the year, since it sets the tone of a class—teachers have to present material so that students will find it palatable. In its highest form, this is called inspiring them, a term literally meaning "giving life to." A word of caution, however. No technique for encouraging student interest and motivation is magic. As the proverbial story of the horse that refused water suggests, finally it is a student himself who must become motivated and who must do the learning.

The First Day of School: Attracting Students to a Course

"Good morning. I am Ms. Doolittle in Room 240. Welcome to junior English. Today I want to outline and describe the various areas of language we will study this year, including literature, composition, vocabulary, and grammar. Then I will state the rules and general procedure for the course so that you can know what to expect. Finally, I hope to give you your texts and make your first assignment in them. . . ." Anyone still reading will recall his disappointment at being subjected to such a dull greeting at the start of a new course. Other teachers, apparently hoping to put students more at ease, spend the first session largely talking about themselves or joking. Still others can't seem to be bothered with an introduction at all; they just start the first day with problem one, page one.

However well intentioned, all of these commonly used tactics miscarry because they don't attempt to interest students in the subject matter. Ironically, these introductions also establish that teachers do make an impression on students the first day, no matter how they spend it. A teacher's concern is how best to convince students that the class will be a good one. Although this task is never easy, it is usually facilitated on opening day because students enter wondering what a class and its teacher will be like. And, as one of my own students remarked, they have selfish motives for wanting teachers to be successful, classes interesting.

The first consideration is that students understand what a teacher is saying about the subject. If this sounds too obvious to need mentioning, one needs only recall how many lectures he has left wondering what in the world the speaker was talking about. Often speakers take for granted that an audience knows more than it does about the subject. The speakers flitter to and fro with their own preoccupations and leave their listeners to struggle or snooze as they choose. What if a speaker had to describe a person to be recognized in an airport? It may well be that one fascinating detail about this man is his passion for argyle socks, but since most men don't allow their socks to show, this detail won't help anyone to spot him. Many lecturers focus on just such baffling details. They expound, so to speak, about the color of the socks, their fabric, their size, and their quality without ever describing the man's most obvious features such as his physique. If listeners have any idea of what is meant, they don't know why it's important. Even more bewildering are speakers who use high-flown or obscure language to describe such minutiae. It's as if they're afraid they won't sound erudite if they don't sound complex.

Actually, the more complex an issue, the more simplicity is needed in order for an audience to grasp at once what is being conveyed. This is especially true of introductory sessions, because listeners are confronted with unfamiliar material. Consider an introduction for a course in American history from the Revolution to the Civil War. To a teacher who has recently taken four or five courses in American history, it may seem elementary to contrast the administrations of Madison, Monroe, and Jackson as he introduces his material. To most high school students, however, these names will be meaningless. They will probably just count the names they have to memorize. In all likelihood, the students will have no clear idea of what history itself is, even though that is a term they have heard and used often enough. Most of them will laugh at the idea that their getting out of bed yesterday can be defined as an historical event just as much as George Washington's being our first president. Beyond that, most students assume that the idea of George Washington's being a good president is also historical fact. "Good" is a word they encounter every day, usually without questioning whether it is opinion or fact. Advertisements are very persuasive about one product's goodness, another's greatness, regardless of the validity of their arguments. If students can learn that a judgment about a product is opinion, they can learn that a judgment about Washington or any other person must be opinion as well. Familiar examples such as these help them see that much of what is called history is actually opinion about history; the examples not only define the subject matter but also give students a valid approach to any history book they will ever encounter. Further, they will understand that history is not totally removed from their own lives.

As odd as this may seem, students are often surprised at how directly school subjects are related to their own lives; they are almost always curious about such connections. If the subject is chemistry, for instance, one that many students may think remote, certain ideas can make it more approachable even on the first day. Do they know that chemistry not only makes human life more convenient, but it also saves lives? They take no-iron synthetic clothing for granted; it is the result of the work of chemists. Any number of modern drugs, from aspirin to various antibiotics, are available because chemists discovered or devised them. Oxygen used in emergencies is provided by chemical laboratories. Moreover, it was not by chance that ancient chemists or alchemists were regarded as magicians; they appeared to work wonders. Modern students also see a "magician" when a chemistry teacher produces fire by mixing two fluids. A subject is not cheapened by its sensational characteristics, and it is just those sensational elements that often trigger students' imaginations more quickly than anything else.

Current controversial issues usually interest students too. However, most of them don't realize that a great many controversies in the news now were also debated in times past. Students often think that reading books from earlier ages won't be enjoyable because they assume that books about those times won't have meaning for anybody today. Suppose a teacher is introducing a course in English that will include Melville's *Billy Budd*. Among other things, that novel focuses on capital punishment. It also questions whether the circumstances surrounding a crime or merely the crime itself should be considered in determining guilt or innocence. Should one man be excused for murdering another because his victim had unjustly accused him of mutiny? Since these issues are as alive today as they were when Melville wrote the book in the late nineteenth century, they help students see the universality of human existence in all ages. Of course, *Billy Budd* is about much more than these issues, but an opening session should pose questions to which students will want to find answers.

The tried analogy of the forest and trees is apt. An introductory session usually shouldn't reveal the entire forest because the very comprehensiveness of an overview can be overwhelming. Nor should an introduction be devoted to the bark of any particular tree; its obscurity will make that detail appear irrelevant initially. Both the overview and the details must be saved for a time when students can appreciate them. An introductory session best highlights a number of interesting trees, which attract without overpowering.

At the end of the first day, students should feel that the information of the course will be useful to them practically or that the task will be one they will enjoy mastering anyway. In some courses like home economics and shop, rewards can be immediate and tangible. More often, though, the prize will not be a material one. Students will still want to learn the information if they sense its usefulness. A student knows that he needs good arithmetic skills whenever he purchases anything. However, he may be unable to see the practicality of learning something as abstract as algebra, and he may not know or remember that people enjoy learning all sorts of things that have no practical consequence for them at all. How many students of art in high school become professional artists? Nevertheless, many others enjoy seeing a work they have created. If an algebra student can be shown that problems are puzzles, he won't be concerned about the impracticality of algebra. A teacher doesn't have to promise falsely that learning will be fun; rather he may suggest the pleasure that awaits those who struggle through the puzzle.

An effective introduction, then, must define, intrigue, and promise, and it must do all of these succinctly. Since our attention span for hearing about unfamiliar topics is short, admistrators usually allot less time for introductory sessions than for later periods. "Short" in this case, though, means anything but insignificant. If students leave a class disappointed on the first day, their teacher may well be unhappy about their performance for the rest of the year.

The other mandatory task on the first day is roll call. A seemingly negligible chore, nevertheless it is the first thing students see and hear a teacher do. It is also a job that often proves embarrassing for both students and teacher. Each teacher is faced at the beginning of a year with numerous unfamiliar names. His difficulty is compounded if he is working in a locality where he has not lived before. Imagine a southerner confronted with Mnochubalis, Mozubhekian, and Mraovicz, all on the same roster; those three make Zazzali, Zizzo, and Zuraski seem like child's play. Most students are gracious about a mispronunciation the first time, but not for long. Therefore, letting them say their own names on the first several days has advantages. First, they are doing something rather than simply listening to their teacher. Second, a teacher hears the preferred pronunciation of the name before he attempts it. Third, he can learn the given names by which his students wish to be known. To hear his teacher call "Francis" can be mortifying to a teen-ager who sees himself as "Frank."

Sometimes teachers have students make an introductory remark about themselves as well, since this can help a group to relax. It also aids a teacher in identifying various personality types in his room. However, the technique backfires quickly unless a teacher draws students out with leading questions. Even if they've been on an African safari the previous month, they'll probably say they did nothing; without prompting, many high school students are too self-conscious in a new environment to say even a sentence or two about themselves.

Obviously with so much to accomplish on opening day, there is usually no time to talk about rules and procedures. Nor need a teacher be apprehensive that if he fails to lay down the law on the first day, students will consider him a pushover. It is true that students test new teachers more than they do experienced ones. After all, new teachers are unknown quantities, and often students will say or do things on the first days to see how their teacher responds. A group of girls, for instance, might burst into the classroom five minutes late. If the teacher is unprepared for the test, he will invite confusion. He himself should be certain of the rules and procedures by which the class will operate, but formal announcements about these matters overemphasize the threat of punishment rather than convey the excitement of learning.

Furthermore, rules are only effective when all violators are punished, and punished uniformly. That means that when a teacher establishes a rule he must be certain that he has both the authority and the desire to punish all offenders. If he pronounces that each student late to class will have to make up the time after school, the teacher must not only stop the lesson to take note of those tardy, but he must also remain with them after school. It often happens that the longer a person teaches, the fewer rules he announces in the beginning. This does not mean that a teacher is lazy or that he tolerates disruptive behavior. He simply knows that students will test his rules. He also knows that high school students understand the kind of behavior that is expected of them. Most students realize that they are supposed to be punctual, prepared, and attentive. They know they are not supposed to disrupt a lesson. Individual teachers really do not have to establish formal rules about appropriate classroom behavior even though they realize that their students, like all people, will not always do what they should. If an offense is not habitual or egregious, it may be better for all concerned to overlook it. Besides, opening day is the time to remind students of what they can do rather than to force them to hear about what they can't.

Distributing texts and assignments, another common use of opening day, is also ineffective unless there is ample time to prepare students for what they are getting. It is not a job simply to fill time. Since schools, not students, usually buy the books, most high school texts are necessarily used for a number of years. Even if the edition has been attractively published, it will be dirty, torn, and underlined by the time it reaches most of its users. Further, the books are frequently big and heavy, and as students know all too well from experience, the writing in most is extremely dull. What person could possibly want such a "present" on the first day of school, especially if he is instructed to read the first chapter by the next day? Distributing books also takes time, and while this time is not wasted, it is time lost to instruction. Before teachers assign books, they should prepare students to want them, or barring this, at least not to toss them aside in disgust.

Perhaps the best way a teacher could evaluate the effectiveness of an introductory session would be to switch places mentally with a student in the class. A teacher would then ask himself whether he would be eager to study in the course. Does it sound interesting or worthwhile? Should he try to change courses? If a teacher's answers to fundamental questions like these are scarey, at the least they will prepare him for the way others will feel about the course; at the best they may direct him to positive change.

Keeping Students Interested Throughout the Year

According to most analysts, television is conditioning viewers to expect instant gratification. When a program ceases to please, they simply switch the dial to another channel—apparently most don't switch the TV off. Students are usually unable to change teachers or courses when they find that for some reason they don't like one. However, students can tune out just as effectively as if they were no longer in the room. Preventing this not only benefits them but also serves a teacher's self-interest. Even when there are no overt discipline problems, supervising a group of rocks posing as students can disconcert a teacher.

In fact, teachers have to be performers. The extent to which their classroom "performances" are successful is partly an accurate measure of students' interest in subjects. One college professor of mine devoted her classes solely to lectures; acually she read her material to us in a muffled monotone. While her analyses of the French Revolution may have been penetrating, all I remember of the course was this rather pathetic woman herself. Had she been teaching in a high school, her pupils probably would not have remained as quiet as we did, but our stupor was surely more debilitating for her than any noise could ever be. While our yawns and slouches and glazed eyes must have told her that no one was listening, she apparently felt it her duty to carry on. Most likely, she simply didn't know what else to do.

In learning to become accomplished public speakers, teachers can do no better than study the technique of a successful comedian, not because teachers have to be funny, but because a comedian is one speaker who never forgets his audience. After telling a joke that falls flat, he will almost always stop and acknowledge the failure of his story. Invariably listeners laugh louder at his confession than at his joke, but they are laughing *with* him, not *at* him. Happy that he has remembered them, that he wants them with him, they become more cooperative.

Whether called on to laugh or not, any audience cues the speaker in a number of ways about his effectiveness. To be unresponsive to their prompting conveys that they are insignificant. If a teacher is explaining something or leading a discussion and notices that most students of a class are "asleep," his first priority should be to wake them up. This isn't so hard since to startle people sufficiently by any means is to awaken them. The trouble often lies in keeping them awake, as manufacturers of the snooze alarm understand. When students sleep in class, they are usually daydreaming; nobody likes to relinquish a dream for anything less interesting than the dream itself. What if a teacher slips in something these dreamers will see as important, though, such as information about the next day's exam? Almost without exception they sense when something's happened they shouldn't have missed, and their perplexity frequently brings them to life.

In addition to being alert to their audience, public speakers must acquire considerable technical skill to be forceful. Using a tape recorder can be helpful. The material taped can be any that the individual feels comfortable with. For instance, he might try reading from a favorite book or magazine or asking a friend to record an informal conversation with him. I do not recommend taping actual class sessions since that often puts undue pressure on both students and teacher.

If one practices with this device, though, he should recall that a taped voice always sounds distorted to the speaker himself. Of course, the method is also incomplete. It cannot reveal volume, a prime consideration about any speech, since a touch of a knob corrects that. Moreover, it cannot show whether a speaker has sufficient eye contact with all members of the audience. It's tempting when one speaks to a group to look primarily at persons who are most responsive to what is being said. By doing this a speaker may be looking primarily at the extroverts in a group and ignoring everybody else.

For all the method's incompleteness, there are two distinct advantages of hearing oneself on tape. First, the pace of a speech becomes apparent. More people tend to rush their words than to speak too slowly; this habit proves embarrassing if a person thinks he has prepared a half-hour presentation only to find himself with nothing to say after fifteen minutes. A normal conversational pace is also the most appropriate one for public speaking because it allows an audience enough time to think about what is being said. The reason it is often so difficult to listen to someone read a speech is that a reader goes too fast for the audience to keep up with him. He doesn't have to think about what he's saying, and he doesn't have to search for words. Those pauses when a speaker is thinking are necessary because they provide time for a listener to think as well.

Knowing when to pause is important in pacing too. I am always amused but annoyed when I hear one radio announcer in a rural community read the weather report: "Today will be [an approximately five-second pause follows] cold. Tonight the temperature [five seconds] will drop to [two seconds] fifteen. Tomorrow we expect [two seconds] the cold to continue. . . ." I usually become so impatient with him that I can't hear his facts for listening to his pauses. A native speaker of English expects pauses in a sentence at the end of a thought. Verbs must follow their subjects without interruption, as must complements their verbs. To have to wait unnaturally even for a few seconds directs attention to how something is said rather than to what is said.

A tape also reveals whether a voice conveys enthusiasm for its subject. No one will listen for long to anyone who does not project some excitement about what he is saying. Even though this may seem a strange admission about teachers, they sometimes seem uninterested in their disciplines. One math teacher I know would really be happier teaching English. And what if an English teacher likes novels, doesn't especially enjoy poetry, and can't abide grammar and punctuation? Enthusiasm for a subject is difficult for teachers to fake because most of them aren't professional actors; sincerity or lack of it shows in their voices and expressions. If a teacher projects true enthusiasm for his subject, on the other hand, that enthusiasm alone can stimulate otherwise apathetic students. At least they see that someone is excited about the subject.

Some teachers attempt to enliven classes by trying to be funny. The key word here is "trying," though, rather than "funny"; the corniness that results from trying to be funny often deserves groans more than laughter. Of course, simple humor has the advantage that almost everyone understands it. Used sparingly, and to help a group relax, it usually conveys that a teacher is friendly, but unless a class is entirely confident of a teacher's competence, such jokes can misfire. A substitute teacher once tried to amuse a history class by spelling Karl Marx's name "Marks." Because the students didn't know the substitute, they weren't sure whether they were supposed to laugh at him. Adults would probably have given this speaker the benefit of the doubt, but even pianist-comedian Victor Borge says that during his clowning he always plays one difficult piece correctly.

To be successful with stories, one has to know where to start them, what details to include, and how to pace them. He must also understand the level of sophistication of the audience. Often a teacher finds that students don't enjoy many of the same stories he does, especially subtle puns. If a few students don't understand the punchline, they will feel stupid and embarrassed even though they may laugh rather than admit they don't understand. When it happens that most people in a class don't get the point, they simply think the teacher foolish. They may indulge him by saying something like, "Guess you had to be there to get it," but they still think the teacher either doesn't know what's funny or doesn't know how to tell a story.

Students usually adore teachers who laugh frequently and who understand how to make others laugh. Laughter suggests that a person is happy even if he's not. Students flocked to the classes of one teacher because they had heard from other students that she was very funny. Some actually told her after the first class that they were disappointed she hadn't told any jokes. What they came to discover was that she was funny not because of any prepackaged stories she told but because of her spontaneous quips, mannerisms, and mimicry.

Whether or not it is desirable educationally, most high school students work primarily for a teacher rather than to master a subject. One often hears remarks like, "Oh, I had to do a good job on that paper because my teacher would have been so disappointed in me if I hadn't." Or, conversely, "I don't care when I get that assignment in, the teacher's so crazy." For a teacher to set out directly to try to make students like him would probably be as obvious to them as it was odious. However, when one thinks about why he likes another person, especially a teacher, it is frequently because that person takes a friendly interest in him. Teachers must learn a great deal about their students in relation to their subjects if they want to help them improve. Students also appreciate being noticed personally in ways quite apart from the subject, although many teachers seem to feel that they shouldn't do this. Like everybody, students enjoy hearing that they look attractive or that they've done something thoughtful or outstanding.

Beginning teachers will find, too, that because of their own youth, students will be predisposed to like them. A new teacher with natural talent for his trade and with confidence in that talent quickly becomes popular with students. They admire teachers who can make them do what they're supposed to but who are also young enough to like the same things they do. Even perky middle-aged teachers, not to speak of older ones, will always seem a little old-fashioned to teen-agers because they're old enough to be their parents. Most of these teachers don't dance the latest dances or sing the current hits. They probably don't even know what those dances and songs are. At the same time, sharing mutual interests can make students envious of young teachers. A teacher may well be wearing the clothes and driving the car that students want but can't afford.

If a new teacher is unsure of himself, his age quickly becomes a detriment to his work. Students take advantage of uncertainty in teachers, and they often test competency before teachers know what has happened. Suppose an uninhibited boy or girl inquires what his new teacher did prior to coming to the school. Learning that his teacher is holding his first job may be as unsettling to the student as going under the knife of an inexperienced surgeon would be to a patient. Unlike the patient, the student may not wish to run away, but supposedly in all innocence he has obtained personal information that may influence his esteem of his teacher.

Techniques That Foster Motivation

Given interesting teachers, students are apt to be attentive to the subject. Their willingness to exert themselves sufficiently to actually learn it is another matter. Most people would like to be able to do many things they somehow never get around to mastering. How many adolescents who would like to play the guitar never bring themselves to learn how? Ironically, one sure method for encouraging motivation isn't used in schools. Although everybody acknowledges that people as well as other animals always want what they are denied, deprivation would seem incongruous in the classroom. Fortunately, other techniques also spur students to work.

When a teacher selects the material for a course, he is guided by several considerations. He takes into account what is usually expected of persons who have studied this subject and what his students already know about the discipline. In addition, a teacher should be guided by material students will find meaningful or enjoyable so that they will have an almost built-in incentive to learn. Most students are attracted to learning anything that seems significant to them, particularly something related to their own lives. Quite apart from the limited immediacy that was the object of much of the outcry in the 1960s for "relevance," the core of what is pertinent to students' lives remains largely unchanged from century to century. Only the trappings around the core change. This explains why, for instance, the questions the classical Greek plays raise about human existence are as applicable today as they were to the Greeks twenty-five hundred years ago. A teacher's task is to help students interpret connections between their own concerns and the material they are being asked to master.

Peculiarly, the more details a person knows about a subject, the less likely he will be to extract from it key ideas that would be interesting and pertinent to those who know less about it. Textbooks, written by experts in a particular field, often tacitly assume that all readers will also want to become specialists. The danger for a teacher is that he's professionally involved in the same area as the text, and he may forget how the subject appears to one who will never become a specialist in that field.

Thus students frequently have to grope their way from one detail to another without ever understanding what those details amount to; they leave a course with little or no comprehension of what the discipline is all about. The forest-and-trees analogy serves once again. Fairly early in a course students should be shown a view of the forest. Although initially they may be unable to grasp very much of the overview, a glimpse of the whole provides a rationale for mastering its various components. Without that, the details, the veins of the leaves so to speak, may appear meaningless. Once students have learned the details, necessarily the most time-consuming part of any course, they should be brought once more to view the whole. Most will be unable to construct the whole for themselves even though they know its components. Still, they will see it with much more appreciation than they did at the beginning of the course. At this point what they have been taught finally makes sense to them.

Suppose the course is one in biology. With no fanfare, each student is set to dissecting his frog and learning its parts. At first that procedure may excite a student because the drama of an operation room is hard to resist. As days become weeks, though, and the reek of formaldehyde permeates everything a student touches, he may well become disgusted with his amphibian "patient." He may not see why he needs to learn all the names, especially the foreign-sounding ones, as well as the locations of bones, nerves, and organs. He's not going to be a scientist, a doctor, or a teacher. He's going to be a realtor. For the student's purposes, Latin and Greek derivatives like epidermis and dermis are no better than the common terms, outer skin and inner skin; the former are simply more confusing. What he wants to learn from his pickled frog are not arbitrary labels that experts have coined to communicate with one another but principles of life. Why will a frog die unless his skin is moist? How does a frog "breathe" through his skin even though lungs are present? It is not that students object to learning difficult material. In fact, names are easier to learn than processes or concepts. Rather students resist learning anything that seems unimportant to them.

Extracting the fundamentals of a subject in a way that students can feel the information is meaningful calls on a teacher's ingenuity as well as his daring. He cannot rely on material being valuable simply because it is suggested in a textbook or because he himself learned it in a given course. A student's prodding may also spur a teacher to change. The first time he hears a student ask, "Why should I learn this?" (a question most teachers eventually hear no matter how it is phrased), his answer may be quite confused. He may feel as parents do the first time their children confront them with one of the "where did I come from?" questions.

Of course, students don't always have all the facts before them when they complain about the impracticality of a subject. They often balk at learning to write because they argue that most people today don't use this skill much after they are out of school. The students are partially correct—most occupations don't require writing beyond perhaps completing an occasional form or so, and the telephone has virtually replaced correspondence. What students don't see, though, is that learning to write well is beneficial even if a person never writes again, since writing is one of the best means of forcing oneself to think precisely. A writer must not only develop his ideas clearly in a certain sequence, but he must also anticipate his reader's objections to his thoughts. This juggling between one's subject, one's self, and one's audience demands a mental dexterity that few other tasks enforce.

Students also resist learning anything that seems totally alien to them. Like travelers, they easily weary of exposure to whatever is wholly new. Conversely, students in a foreign language are always surprised and happy when they discover cognates with their own language. If the Germans say *Haus* and *Mann* and *Auto*, their language is not very different from English; it becomes comprehensible. The principle of association explains as well why students are delighted to learn sources of quotations they have heard all of their lives. Many can't believe at first that Shakespeare wrote "Something is rotten in the state of Denmark," but they're proud of themselves for learning that.

The appeal of a writer like Shakespeare may rest ultimately on his depiction of lifelike characters and on his poetry, but initially it rests on his prestige. Students have heard of him before they get to a course. Even though his plays may be somewhat unintelligible to them at first, they think the struggle's worth it because everybody recognizes Shakespeare's importance. In any subject similar names abound: Einstein, Darwin, Galileo, Napoleon, Freud, Mozart. Students understand that there are some things about which every educated person should be informed.

The more a teacher builds on what students know when they enter a new course, the more successful that teacher will be. In one school an English teacher began a course by having students watch and analyze TV soap operas for a week. While this scandalized some of her colleagues, her students thought that was one of the best units of the entire year. They liked to discuss those shows, and principles of criticism were applied to them just as rigorously as they would have been to an eighteenth-century sentimental drama. No one would suggest that material like this should be the total fare in a course, but students should feel that what they do in school is not entirely separate from what they do the rest of the time.

When a person can see a relationship between what he knows and what he is asked to learn, he feels he has a good chance to succeed. Students always like to find that what they have learned in one course is helpful in another; in this way their academic work is not fragmented. While some courses such as math and science lend themselves naturally to this, teachers often discover other ways to relate various subjects. Suppose an English teacher planned to teach *The Red Badge of Courage* in October. If he discovers that most of his students will not study the Civil War until February, waiting until that time to use the novel will make it more significant for the students. For that matter, if a history teacher knows his students are reading that book in English, he might ask them what it taught them about the war.

Most high school teachers do not and should not give pat lectures, but faced with conveying information to large groups, they frequently resort to doing most of the talking in any class period, since this requires less time than other methods to present material. Moreover, the personal touch of a teacher's explanations allows most people to learn from them more easily than from a textbook, even though his explanations primarily reinforce or expand materials in the textbook. However, lecturing—albeit informal—is also the least effective way of teaching. I once overheard some students discussing a teacher who apparently lectured almost every day. One student said, "All he ever does is talk, talk, talk. When I get there he's talking, and when the bell rings he's still talking." To his students, the teacher's endless monologue had become so much empty noise to endure. Anyway, when a person is told what to think about a subject, it is never as truly his as when he has to figure it out himself by reasoning and/or experimenting. Lecturing might almost be compared to giving a person goods without his having asked for them; often those goods become meaningless. Most teachers, therefore, combine a lecture type of explanation with question-and-answer sessions, discussions, and other experiential methods.

In planning questions, a teacher's key for the first round is simplicity if he expects students to be able to respond. A teacher might be tempted to think students will not esteem him if his questions don't sound sophisticated, but students have read the material or worked the problems only once, and then hastily. Questions like "What do you think the author is trying to say?" or "What is the significance of that idea?" are too complex; students are wondering what the idea is. Ideally students answer most questions voluntarily, but they won't unless they think they can answer correctly. They should also feel free to ask anything at all about the material they don't understand, but, again, they won't if they think their questions might appear foolish. When a teacher finds himself asking questions only to have to answer them himself, many times that is because his questions are too hard. The first questions should help students grasp the basic facts of the material or reinforce those facts for them. For instance, questions like "What happened?" are appropriate. After that a little more difficult questions can help them see why it happened and, finally, the significance of the occurrence.

A teacher should always answer patiently any student question that is asked sincerely. Frequently a teacher must try three or four approaches before a student understands the explanation. Asking other students who know the answer to share in the teaching is almost always exciting and profitable. It's well to keep in mind, also, that a question does not have to be answered at the moment asked. Sometimes it will fit better in another part of the lesson. Sometimes a teacher needs more time alone to think about the answer. Sometimes he simply doesn't know the answer. That's fine, as long as the question isn't one most students feel he should know. It's one thing for a teacher to convey he's human; it's quite another to convey he's unprepared.

A question-and-answer session is what some teachers actually seem to have in mind when they use the term *discussion*. True discussion must revolve around controversy. Factual questions (for example, Who is the current Secretary of State?) lead to no discussion, even though most factual questions can be reshaped into controversial ones (Is the Secretary of State doing a good job?). A discussion has not occurred if each response is directed to the leader; that's a question-and-answer session. A discussion occurs when the participants respond to each other's ideas. The question remains whether such situations just happen or whether a teacher can create them. The answer is both, to a certain extent.

To provoke stimulating discussion, the teacher should provide an initial question or questions, ones he is fairly confident students will find interesting. Rarely should a teacher begin with, "Now what would you like to discuss about this today, class?" As simple as that question sounds, it's most likely too difficult unless students have thought carefully about the work. It is the teacher also who decides when the discussion should be terminated. Letting everyone have a say, especially when many contributions are virtually identical, is not always the best solution. Too much repetition is boring, regardless of who is talking. Moreover, students should leave discussions with a sense that controversy actually exists; that is sometimes difficult if one side speaks too long.

A good leader must also actively participate in the discussion. It is not so much that he should state his own opinion—many leaders refrain from that—but he must know when to prod students with another question or example to force them to see ramifications of their own as well as opposing views. Thus the discussion leader must understand the rationale for the various sides of the controversy before the discussion begins in order to ensure that those different positions are brought out. Suppose in a discussion on euthanasia one student vehemently maintains that nothing can change his opposition to what he calls murder; he believes that only God should take life. If no one else challenges him—and his appeal to religion will intimidate some students who disagree with him—the leader can always provoke the student into seeing what the implications of his philosophy would mean to him personally. In other words, has that student thought how he might feel were his own mother stricken with terminal cancer? Or, on the other hand, imagine a son tired of caring for his aged mother; were euthanasia legal, perhaps he would just as soon have her out of his way long before she is disabled. Even if one is not opposed to euthanasia on religious grounds, it will always remain controversial because of those vexing questions of who will decide and when. Importantly, the function of discussion is to allow students to understand what the sides of an issue are, not to convince them that one side is right.

When a leader knows a group well enough to predict how most of them will think about a particular issue, he can usually provoke discussion by taking the opposite position. Say the issue is the draft. The teacher announces that he believes all eighteen-year-olds, men and women, should be required to register for military service. That stance—or the directly opposite one, depending on the group—will prompt rebuttals.

Some students naturally like to debate more than others; they usually jump in no matter what the question. It's unreasonable, however, to imagine that everybody in a class will volunteer. Some really won't have an opinion about any given topic, and some will be too timid to speak. A good leader, though, guards against anyone's monopolizing the floor. (That includes the leader, too!) Should a student take over, the most tactful approach is to suggest that someone else seems to want to speak. If no one else does, the leader can shift the question slightly. And if that doesn't help, it's probably time to terminate the discussion; it's already over anyway.

Unfortunately, many times students don't think that very much of substance happens during discussions, even good ones. This may be because the necessarily loose organization of a discussion makes it difficult for students to remember what was said. (A brief recapitulation of the main points the following day is often useful.) Their hesitation about the method may also reflect the fact that since there's no one right answer to controversial issues, students feel that they won't be held accountable for the discussion. Discussions may also be overused in high schools; students never take talking as seriously as an exercise for which they must produce tangible results. As long, however, as a discussion remains lively, a teacher doesn't need to worry about these misgivings. Students learn from provocative discussion and are motivated by it, regardless of how it appears to them.

Students are also motivated to learn whenever the subject appears exciting. They like suspense, they like puzzles, they like competitions. Some people claim that these techniques are gimmicks. Competition especially is frequently singled out as stimulating only a base kind of motivation. Of course, competition can be base if the attitudes of those involved are base. One has to question the motivation of any teacher overly concerned about whether his students are better than those of other teachers, because he may not care as much about what students are learning as about his own ego satisfaction or professional advancement. Obviously competition is also harmful if it is rigged. I heard last year of a third-grader who entered a citywide spelling bee, which he nearly won. He lost because the list of words he had studied was incomplete. Students at another school had studied the several words that made the difference in the contest, and one of those students won. It appears in this case that teachers and schools, as well as students, were competing.

However, in the hands of a fair teacher, competition offers a number of advantages for the classroom. These advantages overrule arguments against competition, most of which are based on half-truths. First, opponents of the method claim that the goal of education should be to attain knowledge, not to beat an opponent. To be sure, knowledge is the true end of all education, but a student will inevitably become frustrated if he seeks this goal directly. How will he know when he has attained knowledge? What is knowledge, anyway? It is not any given problem, book, course, or series of courses. Students are successful in the classroom if they obtain information, something vastly more limited than knowledge. Knowledge or wisdom comes, if it does at all, as a by-product rather than as a goal of education.

Second, it is held that if a person must compete, he should compete against himself rather than against someone else. This reasoning, though, not only begs the question, it also makes the matter too abstract. By its very definition, competition involves two or more people. Further, let's say that a person is trying to learn to play the piano. He may recall that last week or last year he was able to play with a given competence, and he may work never to lose that skill. But how does he know what his future goals are? How can he imagine how well he would like to be able to play next year? If a pianist says simply that he wants to be able to play as well as he can, he has no concrete standard of performance by which he can measure what he does. He would be more specific in his goal if he says he wants to play a piece without striking incorrect notes. But is technical flawlessness the only ingredient of good music? For anything as difficult as interpreting a piece, most of us have to set our goals by what we see or hear someone else do. Of course, we applaud another person's achievement when we say that we would like to equal or better it; thus measuring our own competence against someone else's is not necessarily to arouse antagonism. We simply gain a more concrete idea of what we want to achieve ourselves.

Some skills do appear to lend themselves better than others to competing against oneself. Say a person ran a mile in five minutes last year and wants to do it in four and a half this season. However, is he so much competing against himself as against the clock? The clock gives him an absolute standard by which he may judge himself; without that he's simply running as fast as he can and he doesn't know what he's achieving. Even in situations in which competing against oneself might be possible, it is seldom much fun. If a boy wants to improve his debating skill, he might develop logical arguments for the various sides of any given issue and then try to discredit each of those arguments. Can this ever be as exciting as the dramatic situation in which he has to think on his feet and counter an idea he hasn't expected? If a person knows all the angles of strategy—as he must whenever he competes against himself—the element of the unexpected is eliminated. Usually the peak performance that can be exacted when one has to be prepared for anything is missing also.

Much of the quibbling about competition seems to result from a fear about possible harm to losers. Losing, though, seldom damages a person psychologically, even when the results of the contest can be predicted with certainty. In the past few years I have been attempting to learn chess. My usual opponent has been the boy champion of his school. Because of his skill and long experience with the game, I have had and still have little chance to win our matches. Although I am sometimes discouraged, his strength in no way weakens me. On the contrary, I play a better game than I would have had I been competing with someone who didn't know much more about chess than I.

Obviously it's unhealthy for a person to see himself as a loser, a self-assessment that is often cured only by psychological counseling. The image of "loser," though, is as relative as that of "winner." In a contest of four runners, the one who comes in second might well see himself as a loser, while the contender who comes in third in the race might report that he won third place. Seeing oneself as a winner or a loser is a personality trait derived from causes more innate and basic than could result from any competition in high school. While competitions may well reinforce images, there is an irony here too. If one evades contests altogether, he has no chance of ever becoming a winner.

The clearest advantage of competition in the classroom is that it is a method that works when little else seems to. In one English class students were particularly apathetic about Browning's "My Last Duchess," the poem they were studying. The teacher tried to have them dramatize the situation of the poem, lectured about it, tried to lead them in a discussion of it, but they sat expressionless. Although all the class time allotted for the poem had elapsed, it was evident that the students had not learned anything about it or from it. Then the teacher asked the class to divide into two teams, each one formulating questions about the poem that they would later pose to the other team. Only those questions to which they themselves knew the answer were permitted. All at once the students began to read the poem, to notice

every word. When they started to "play," one side became furious
that a girl on the opposite team knew the answers to all their
questions, and they asked for time to regroup to find more difficult questions. Their pride, as well as their sense of gamesman-
ship, had been evoked. That the members of those teams cared
more about besting each other than they did about understanding the poem for its own sake is clear, but they did learn the
poem.

If a person already has a desire to improve himself, a competitive situation simply provides a kind of added incentive for him.
And two forces are usually better than one in accomplishing a
goal. A motivated drama student may say, "I want to learn the
part of Hamlet as well as I can." If that same student is competing against others for that part in a forthcoming play, he must
say, "I want to learn this part better than any other student." The
added exertion demanded in competition, something even nature
respects by supplying additional adrenalin, often means that a
person has a chance of performing at a higher level than when
he is simply doing his best outside of a competitive situation. In
these instances competition is not merely a negative means to an
end but a positive good in itself.

An essay contest was announced in a history class of interested
and competent seniors. The winner of the competition would be
chosen by secret ballot of the students themselves after each of
them had read all of the essays. To create suspense, as well as to
avoid letting personality be of undue importance in the voting,
each person submitted his paper anonymously. Never had this
excellent class worked more diligently or creatively than they did
for this contest. Some of their results seemed to surprise the
given writers as much as they did the other students. They hadn't
realized they could write that convincingly. These were all good
students to begin with, and whether they won or not, the competition gave them a chance to prove themselves better than they
knew. Incidentally, these students worked for a prize as well as
the accolade of "best," and the teacher was somewhat amazed to
observe the excitement that generated. He had thought seniors
might think a prize was silly, but they were eager to know what

it would be and even offered their own ideas about what would make a good award.

To avoid competition in school or to teach students that it is harmful not only deprives them of the fun of a contest but also leaves them unprepared for the world outside the classroom where they must compete for everything from mates to jobs. Should they really feel guilty for getting a job just because they have thereby prevented others from obtaining that same appointment? Should they think that a person who drives himself to become best is thereby harming others? Rather, shouldn't they appreciate that the kind of disciplined determination needed to realize an ambition to become the best actor of one's generation, or the best medical researcher, or the best physicist, or whatever, frequently results in benefits to others, as well as to the individual himself?

Grades

If competition is anathema to some educators, grades are even more so. In fact, grades are often said to lead to unnatural and unhealthy competition. They focus too much attention on reward and too little on learning. Opponents of grades want students to realize that the true reward of learning is something much more meaningful and more intangible than a grade: a learner's reward should be the pleasure of having mastered a task.

Theoretically that position is almost unassailable. Practically speaking, however, to be able to work simply for the pleasure of having learned requires a maturity difficult to muster. In conversation with a distinguished scientist, I discovered that he was becoming discouraged in his work because he wasn't being acknowledged sufficiently for his endeavors. His experiments were leading him to various new insights, but he found that many of his colleagues were skeptical of his findings, which contradicted generally accepted theories, theories on which those colleagues based their own work. This scientist was able to persevere because he wasn't working primarily for the praise of his fellow researchers; he sought information about how nature actually functions. Nevertheless, such going it alone was a stiff potion even for this man with his sights clearly on what he wanted to accomplish. Is it realistic to expect such development from high school students? Most people look forward to recognition when they have done something well. If their efforts remain unacknowledged, they may well start to wonder whether their trouble is worth it.

To our ancestors the matter of reward and punishment for students appeared simple: those who achieved most sat at the head of the class, and those who were doing poorly often had to wear a dunce cap. Because of its public nature, that procedure is horrifying to many modern educators. They point out that the best students frequently capitalize on their ability and actually work no more than (and sometimes less than) poorer ones. The so-called dunces, on the other hand, may have been incapable of performing the task altogether, or their behavioral problems may have interfered with their learning.

Ironically, for all our attempts to be fair, students themselves persist with the kind of ranking that our predecessors used. There seems to be no way to prevent members of a class from knowing who is excelling and who isn't. Before a teacher can finish returning a set of papers, almost everyone in the room will know who received the superior and inferior marks, even though all the teacher did was to call each student's name. Students see and hear each other's work; the brasher ones directly inquire of others how they are doing. What students are insisting upon is some kind of public recognition or reward for a good performance and denigration of a poor one. And to a certain extent they have not only history but science as well on their side. The "cheese and shock" experiments demonstrate that animals learn quickest when they are rewarded immediately for desirable behavior and punished for undesirable behavior.

Admittedly, grades occasionally encourage undesirable behavior. If a student covets good grades enough, or if his family does for him, he or they might do anything they can to get the desired results. They may question the validity of what is taught as well as how it is taught. They may cajole teachers and administrators, lie, or cheat. In one instance even the president of the student honor society plagiarized a paper to try to get a superior grade. Sometimes, too, teachers are uncertain about which grade is actually the proper one, and the grade given may not be the one earned.

For all the acknowledged problems with grades, there are two very logical reasons why this system doesn't disappear. First of all, learning often ceases to be gratifying because beyond a certain level progress is difficult for an individual learner to ascertain. He may have to go for weeks without really being able to tell whether he's getting anywhere or not. (Teaching is frustrating for the same reason.) A good grade encourages students to continue to struggle in the same direction they have taken. By the same token, a poor grade can be an incentive to improve by changing that direction. Second, evaluation allows for differentiation of students' work. Most students and their parents will demand this differentiation if educators themselves don't. A few years ago many schools experimented with a pass-fail system of evaluation. While at first enthusiastic about what appeared to be to their benefit, many students quickly became disillusioned with P-F because they wanted to know if they had passed with honors, passed with mediocrity, or passed by the skin of their teeth. The P alone meant little or nothing to them, or for that matter to their future employers, since 85 or 90 percent of their fellows also had P's.

The thorniest cases of high school grading involve courses required for graduation. A failing grade in one of those is like a doomsday knell to a senior. I recall vividly one instance from my first year of teaching in high school. The boy was thoroughly affable; he was also quick-witted. I still laugh when I remember his response to a fellow student who regretted our completion of *Grapes of Wrath*. The boy in question was as tired of that novel as I; he told his classmate that if he liked the book that much, he might write a sequel to it called *Sons of Grapes of Wrath*. As clever as he was, though, he didn't complete most of the requirements of the course. Perhaps he thought he wouldn't have to. While he had failed two terms of senior English and had only a D in the third term, by late April he was already accepted at a respected university. After his college acceptance, his classwork ceased altogether.

Nevertheless, when he discovered in late May that he wouldn't pass the course and hence wouldn't graduate, he seemed perplexed. He pleaded with me, as did his father for him. The father wanted a precise list of work his son hadn't mastered. I remember how one item rankled the father. "The semicolon," he howled. "My son doesn't know how to use the semicolon. So what?" Both father and son tried to impress upon me that little was to be gained by forcing the boy to go to summer school. I had to admit that he was innately brighter than many other graduating seniors. However, since he hadn't completed most of the assignments for the course, he hadn't passed the exams. Passing courses in school is not merely a matter of innate ability; passing courses is also a matter of completing requirements. Maybe he learned this by having to attend summer school. Anyway, there was no way I could have passed him and been fair to his fellow students who had worked.

To prevent some of that kind of unpleasantness, I've learned to do several things. No student should be surprised by either a term grade or a final grade. They need a more constant reminder of their standing in a course than tests and papers administered every two or three weeks can provide. My students give themselves weekly a letter grade on their effort in class participation. I encourage them to justify with a sentence or two why that grade is deserved. If I agree with their evaluation, all I need do is initial their report; if I disagree I indicate why. At the beginning of a year, I as often have to raise as lower grades. Students appreciate the idea of a grade on effort, and their brief comments, as well as my addenda, keep their progress before them. Second, they and I calculate their term and final grades. This is easy for them to do if they understand what percentage of the total grade each item of work counts. They really should be given these percentages at the outset of a course because that can help them decide how much effort to invest in a given assignment. At the end of a term, students enjoy figuring their averages, and the process means that any errors are caught before grades are officially reported. Although students often wish they had earned a higher grade, the figures convince most of them that their mark is just.

We shouldn't leave the subject of grades without some discussion of the individual assignments and tests on which they are based. Because testing is an incentive to most students to study, it has been suggested that their motivation for learning will increase if a test itself also forces them to learn. As convincing as that idea sounds, time alone makes it an impossibility. A test is constructed for students to demonstrate mastery of material. Learning must occur before a test or after it.

Most likely when people say that students should learn on tests, they actually have something else in mind. They probably mean that a test should require more than memorization of disconnected facts; it should also demand understanding of what those facts mean. For example, if students were being tested on *Macbeth,* they would demonstrate that they knew some of the facts of that play if they knew that Macbeth personally killed or arranged for murder on four different occasions. At a deeper level they would show knowledge of ideas if they knew something of Macbeth's personal values. Understanding would be required if students had to reveal relationships among those facts. Suppose they were asked the extent to which Macbeth's personal values changed after each of his murders. Students enjoy a question like that because it gives them a chance to show off what they have learned. Most of them realize that while assimilation of facts may be a difficult feat, it is seldom as demanding or respected as understanding of those facts.

Whether understanding should be taught before it is tested is also a worthwhile consideration. Several years ago a class of mine objected to my tests, which they said consisted of questions they had already mastered in lectures or discussion. The students felt it was important for each person in the class to formulate his own ideas about the meaning of a book rather than meekly adopting what others said as true. They believed that the best way to accomplish this was for them to write about a work before it was studied in class. I agreed to construct appropriate questions. Almost as soon as their plan was effected, however, some of those students discovered that they had neither time, interest, nor ability to prepare for the tests. They didn't feel adequate to write about a book merely because they had read it, and the published critical accounts from which they sought help often turned out to be less meaningful to them than classwork. Originally all but one boy had voted for the new procedure. At the end of the year, the group was evenly divided. I encouraged them to discuss the method's advantages and disadvantages with students in the following year's class. When the time came for the new group to vote, all but two wanted to write about a work after it had been discussed in class. They apparently realized that as much as we may aspire to independent thought, it is extremely difficult to formulate.

This is not to say there is no place for evaluations that encourage creativity. They challenge students to think, they are usually more interesting to read, and they are one way teachers have of recognizing their most gifted students. Suppose a history class was being tested on Franklin's *Autobiography*. While the class had discussed Franklin's personal characteristics shown in that work, it had not evaluated which of those traits contributed most to his success in business, politics, and science. A question asking students to attempt the latter would interest them more than one asking them to substantiate a certain number of Franklin's traits. Nevertheless, even a well-prepared and independent thinker would find himself at a disadvantage with a question like that if he had not previously considered what traits generally lead to success. One way to be fair is to allow full credit to students demonstrating adequate mastery of the material, regardless of how convincing they may be on the twist of the question demanding originality. Another solution is to announce the question in advance of the test session so students can think about their answers. When they are given time to prepare, they can be further spurred by understanding that the teacher will match the care of his evaluation to the care of their preparation.

Authorities disagree considerably about just how difficult tests should be. It is always possible to construct a question so complex that no one could answer it satisfactorily. If that seems futile, one respected view of testing is that a question is satisfactory when only 50 percent of those tested answer it correctly. At the opposite extreme, some hold that if material has been properly taught and thoroughly studied, there's no reason why all students shouldn't answer a question correctly. From a student's perspective, the best tests are probably those that make them think without overwhelming them. I remember a particular test in college that confounded me. While I was taking it, I felt miserable because I realized how poorly I was doing. I had no way of knowing that everybody else in the room was as frustrated as I. It turned out that 49 was the top grade; my score of 42 received an A-. Still, that grade didn't make me feel much better than I had the day I took the exam. I wondered why none of us knew those questions if the teacher felt we should. At the time I concluded that the subject was simply impossibly complex. Now I recognize that the test was not constructed for beginners in that subject; even specialists probably couldn't have answered all of those questions.

To construct good tests, teachers often start by writing out answers rather than questions—that is, they start with information students should know and then devise questions that can elicit that information. The form a question takes is less important than the precision of its wording. Students usually assume that the objective forms of tests, such as multiple-choice, true-false, and matching, are the easiest since they demand recognition rather than recall. However, while those tests occasionally penalize a student who has reasoned beyond their limited scope, they can also demand exactitude impossible with other forms of testing. A person either knows the material or he doesn't. If he's allowed to write an answer, he may be able to camouflage lack of knowledge with words. Teachers learn quickly, though, that even essay questions must be worded objectively if the answers to them are to be graded fairly.

A variety of types of tests in all subjects is probably the approach that benefits students most. Too often they lack sufficient experience with objective tests in courses in the humanities. Many complain when they face the advanced placement tests in history

and literature; they feel that a knowledge of something like poetry can't be tested objectively. What they are really troubled
about, though, is the care in reading that those tests demand. On
the other hand, when students are tested primarily with objective
forms, as frequently happens in science courses, they get too
little experience with writing. An extreme case was a Ph.D. candidate who had not been required to write a single essay examination or paper from the time he graduated from high school
until he began to prepare his dissertation.

A teacher counts himself lucky indeed on testing days if all
students are present. Since absentees have a way of finding out
what was tested, make-up tests should differ from the original.
Most teachers also construct a more difficult test the second time
around. When students understand this, they may complain that
they should all be measured by a similar standard. They may
also point out that a difficult make-up test is unfair to students
with legitimate absences. Students have to understand, though,
that there are consequences for almost any circumstance, even
those over which a person has no control. I mention to my
students the case of an athlete who was unable to do his best in a
game because of an illness. Everybody who knew him felt sorry
for him, but nobody thought the game was unfair. Aside from
what I tell my students, I know that teachers have to think of
their own time and energy too. If a teacher is to protect himself
against a constant barrage of malingerers, word must travel that
the original test was easier than the make-up.

After a test is over, some students start to beg right away for
their grades; a teacher often feels as if he's being constantly pes-
tered to evaluate papers. From the students' point of view, they
simply want to know how they did while they can still remember
exactly what they did. What would happen if a singer had to
wait two weeks after his performance for applause or boos? He
would be unable to remember exactly how he had sung. What
was it specifically that he should continue to do, and what should
he change?

When papers are returned to students, their first thought is for
their grade. But if that's all they notice about a paper, teachers

have largely wasted their time in grading it. To improve, students must be helped to analyze where they excelled as well as what they did wrong. In the beginning of a course, I sometimes devote as many as three class periods after a test for a theoretical discussion of the test questions. I am emphatic that no individual test papers will be considered during this time. Students are first asked to list points that should be included in the answers. Then they read several duplicated answers printed anonymously but selected to demonstrate either different approaches to the answers or different degrees of success. Students also assign a grade to each answer. Finally we discuss the merits as well as the weaknesses of each response. Students can see the way in which good essay answers are formulated. My students say the procedure convinces them that even essay questions can be graded objectively.

Sometimes a large portion of the class misses a question on a test. When that happens and especially when their incorrect answers are identical, a teacher should look carefully at the question before returning the papers. Students have a right to know why they missed any given question, and if a teacher can't explain that logically, the validity of the entire test may be undermined. A question may be at fault; it's virtually impossible to weed out all poor ones before a test is administered the first time. Students are understanding about that as long as they are not penalized for what is the teacher's error. By the way, many teachers find it helpful to take a test themselves before giving it to students. This forces a teacher to scrutinize the wording of a test and it also allows him to gauge the time required to take it.

Irrespective of a question's merit, students like to quibble about what they have missed. If they see that a teacher is wavering about a question, they will try to point out ambiguities in its wording, as well as the logic of their answers. "Wouldn't it theoretically be possible to look at the question this way?" they ask. "Shouldn't I be allowed some credit because I said this?" Although students like to argue these fine points before the entire class, I avoid such a situation. It is often difficult for a teacher to think clearly about the issue with everybody looking on. Because of that and because individual answers are the concern only of the author and the teacher, most teachers postpone these discussions for a private session with the individual concerned.

Horses Won't Always Drink

One October after I had been teaching for two years, I was quite taken aback to hear a highly respected and experienced teacher tell me that he dreaded to go to his tenth-period class. When I asked why, he said that the students in that period were noisy and ignorant and seemed satisfied to remain that way. No matter what he tried to do to excite them about the subject, they just sat and stared. The reason his admission startled me was I had somehow assumed that after teaching for a time one would eventually learn how to reach all or most of his students. Here was a much revered teacher saying that it simply doesn't happen this way. Apparently even the best of teachers can expect to have unsuccessful classes from time to time because successful classes do not depend solely on the skill of a teacher.

There is a difference, of course, between lack of attention and lack of motivation, but as long as either of these conditions persists students won't learn much. Teachers have to accept that even their most dedicated and eager students will often be inattentive. No one really understands why a person's mind races so from subject to subject, but concentration is something few achieve for very long. Maybe the teacher's nose all of a sudden reminds a student of the dog he saw the previous night, and that association leads to another. The student may hear nothing else from the outside world until the bell startles him from his daydream. Besides this, students have various personal reasons for being inattentive. If they are hungry or if anything hurts, they probably won't be able to concentrate regardless of what a teacher does. At other times, they may simply be savoring a date, a dance, a song, or whatever.

Moreover, any student wants to appear well before his friends, and he will usually stop work instantly to listen to any one of them. If he misses his work, he can make it up, but his friend may not wait. Anyway, it appears that TV commercials are conditioning us all to think we really don't need to listen the first time something is said. We'll surely hear it repeated if we're really supposed to get it.

Apart from inattentiveness, the reasons students lack motivation are as numerous as students themselves. Various persons, including parents and friends, play a part. Also, a student's own past academic achievement is influential. By the time a student reaches high school, he has already had some taste of most of his subjects, and his past experience greatly affects his feeling about a new course, especially in the beginning. A student who has excelled in math previously will be much more motivated than someone who comes to the course feeling "math and I just don't get along." In classes of students grouped heterogeneously according to ability, teachers find that many more students enter classes feeling negatively about the subject than positively. The same is true if a class is a homogeneous group of average or below-average ability.

There are also students who, while they may not particularly dislike a subject, haven't progressed enough in similar courses to allow them to be enthusiastic about a new one. These feelings are especially likely to occur in classes in which students are asked to refine previously acquired skills rather than to learn new ones as, for example, in much language instruction. Because most students are given some kind of instruction in English every year, by the time they reach twelfth grade they may well have a sense of *déjà vu*. They can anticipate reading different books and writing on different topics, but they may not think that they will really be learning how to read or write better. The validity of their view doesn't matter either; their holding it will initially make them uninterested in a new course in the area.

For teachers to blame themselves unnecessarily when students are ininattentive or unmotivated is a waste of time and emotion, for it is, after all, an individual student who must change these conditions. Teachers can't do it for him. All they can do is try to conduct the kind of class in which uninterested students will at least be tempted to reverse their feelings about the subject.

When students don't seem to be taking to a course as a teacher wishes, it may improve matters to consult outside the classroom with three or four students individually. The point to ascertain from each is why he personally is uninterested—it is never really a student's concern as to why a class as a whole isn't working. If a teacher selects students who are intelligent and fair-minded, he can sometimes learn why persons who normally would be motivated aren't. Suppose a teacher is presenting information more quickly than students can absorb it. An accelerated pace can impede them more than the boredom that accompanies a pace that is too slow. More often than not, the condition isn't so easily remedied, and if a teacher doesn't know what's wrong, most likely the students won't know either, or if they do they will be unwilling to explain why to the teacher. It may be that the personalities of the students in the room don't blend; they may actually despise being together. Whatever, students don't see that it is their concern to make a teacher's task easy. It may be they who suffer ultimately if they don't learn the material, but this isn't usually on their minds when problems arise in a classroom. If they see that a teacher cannot reach them—in other words, cannot do his job—it's too bad for that teacher. Why should they do their job and learn if the teacher can't do his and teach?

To discuss with an entire class why it isn't motivated, as some experts advise teachers to do, only confuses the issue. Classes are never unmotivated; certain individuals in a group are uninspired to work. Such a discussion is actually a public confession to students that a teacher doesn't know how to teach. He is really pleading for students to tell him what to do since he can't think of the right thing himself. It is doubtful whether anyone can respect a person who feels this helpless. The kinder students in a class may feel sorry for a teacher like that, but even they cannot revere him, something students must do if they are to learn from a teacher.

If teachers take their work seriously, they want to succeed all of the time. But isn't this really an unattainable ideal in human affairs and in nature? If they sincerely want to help students, teachers will surely inspire some of them, regardless of methods. When I first began teaching I had classes in which I felt that I hadn't reached any of the students. I was surprised to have some of these same students return from college the next year and thank me for what they had learned in the course.

It is always difficult for a teacher to tell when he has done a good job in the classroom because sometimes the most important things he teaches, such as disciplined study habits, aren't direct parts of the subject matter. Also, since there is no exact measure of good teaching, a teacher's students and colleagues may not hold him to the same standard by which he measures himself. Any teacher who is dissatisfied with what he thinks he is able to achieve might enjoy a humorous suggestion of one of my teachers. Even though he was speaking about discipline instead of motivation, his words apply to virtually all areas of teaching. He always advised teachers that when things didn't seem to be working out as they wished, it was best to stay in their rooms and keep the doors shut.

III
Recognizing and Insisting: Matching Performance with Capacity

Each September a teacher has about a hundred students assigned to him. Some of the pupils won't be ready for the class. Others may be altogether incapable of the work. Some will be eager, many unmotivated or lazy. With that many students, how does a teacher ever recognize who is who?

Most teachers would be overwhelmed if they did not soon learn to distinguish categories of students. Although each person is somewhat unique, all classes, including homogeneous ability groupings, have four main types of students: incapable, unwilling, average, and superior. Understanding the characteristics of these groups not only helps a teacher know with whom he is dealing, but it also helps him understand what he can require. If a student is truly incapable, no amount of urging will change his situation. Nor can a teacher compel students to do anything they really don't want to. Rather a teacher tries to show them how to develop their capabilities and encourages them to want to do what they can and should be doing. A teacher's goal is that each student's achievement equals his capability.

Students Unable to Learn

Educators often seem uncomfortable about forthright discussion of students who have difficulty in learning. Nothing shows this more clearly than educational jargon for mentally handicapped persons. For a while they were disguised as "educables," an almost unpronounceable adjective-noun that could apply to any student in school. The ones for whom the term was intended, though, were taught in "special education" classes. "Special" led eventually to "exceptional," even though that word had originally designated very gifted students. To spare the recent breed of "exceptional" students any stigma of being different from others, they were "mainstreamed" into regular classes. (We don't usually mention that eliminating separate classes also saves money.)

In a way I participated in this kind of deception for a while. When I first began to teach composition, I was embarrassed to tell a student explicitly that his ideas were trite. I would mark comma faults and grammatical errors without so much as a twinge, but to criticize a person's thought seemed too personal, too devastating. I remember the first time a student confronted me about this. She didn't understand why her grade was never higher than a C since I didn't comment much about her work. She reminded me that her older sister had gotten A's and B's on her papers and I had written all over them. I had to tell this girl that her ideas were neither well conceived nor developed. I blushed; she didn't. She merely replied, "Oh, ideas. I've never gotten those. I never will." I cannot claim that she learned from me to think more precisely, although I did try to help her with leading questions about her work. However, I learned something very important from her: limited students realize all too well that they are incapable of many of the same things others do.

For teachers to deny disability of any kind or to double-talk about it only confuses students. Sometimes their limitation is so general that it affects them in all of their courses. At other times a very specific function is involved. Each teacher has to determine whether any limitation affects what he is teaching and if it does what his reaction should be.

Here's a typical situation a teacher might face: a general-math student can't work simple written problems involving division. Although the reasons for this may be many, a teacher usually starts by checking prerequisite skills, since they are simpler to measure than motivation or capacity. Ironically, finding out that one student can't divide doesn't carry an automatic solution for a classroom teacher. He has to consider the number of other students in the class who share the same difficulty. If most of the others lack the background material, most likely the objectives for the group should be changed. If only two or three lack the prerequisite, responsibility for make-up work often has to rest largely upon them, with additional instruction arranged if possible. Importantly, when a teacher sets those students to the prerequisite task, he can never be certain that they will be able to master it. All he knows is that they will be unable to progress without it.

Suppose, though, a student is adequately prepared for a course and still can't grasp the work. The general-math student can solve the arithmetical equation of $187 \div 4$ but is stumped by a written problem asking for the cost of a quarter pound of butter if the cost of a full pound is \$1.87. If he is coached enough to be able to work this problem, he may be perplexed anew when he is asked how far one can go in an hour if four hours are needed to go 100 miles. Although he can read all of the words in the problems, he sees no connection between how much butter costs and how long it takes to go somewhere. The ability to see underlying similarities between problems or situations that outwardly appear different is one determinant for success in any course requiring abstract reasoning. If a student lacks that ability, he will always have trouble with written problems because each one will appear entirely different to him. It has been recognized through the ages that teaching is not a matter of giving students capacity; rather, if they have capacity to begin with, teachers supply contexts in which it can be used and developed.

How can a teacher know the limits of any student's ability? is the logical question at this point. The answer is that he can't. How far an individual's capacity can be stretched is always partly a matter of discovery in a particular circumstance; many factors other than innate capability come into play. If a teacher questions whether a student can learn the subject, the teacher should first examine the results of various standardized tests. Most schools have students take a battery of these, and while they are imperfect they do indicate general verbal and quantitative capacity. A student's earlier academic record is also informative. In addition, some schools have specialists who diagnose students' abilities.

A severe mental handicap, often apparent in a person's expression, his movement, and his language, is the exception, not the rule. The very unusualness of most of these cases directs a teacher's attention to them. Most high school students have to struggle to learn the work of most of their courses. For a student to claim he can't understand something or that something is too hard for him usually has nothing to do with incapacity.

It used to be that incapacitated pupils were kept back in the lower grades and largely ignored there. Today too many are ignored in quite a different way: they are passed regardless of what they learn. If that is obviously undesirable, what should teachers do? Probably a consultation with an immediate supervisor is the best starting place. Is a more appropriate class available for the student? If there isn't, the teacher is faced with the following alternatives. He can treat the incapacitated student like everybody else in the class. This, however, not only blocks the student's immediate success but also discourages him about future learning. A second alternative is to assign the same amount of work to all students but to grade it differently. Since the student will be unable to do much of the work, that solution is less effective than a third tack: coaching the student privately and varying the complexity of his work. This third approach takes less of a teacher's time, too, than might at first appear, simply because he is seldom assigned more than one or two such students, if that many, in any term.

In addition to students generally incapacitated, some students have dysfunctions that affect only particular skills. Suppose a tone-deaf girl enrolls in a vocal music class. Since she's going to be a misfit in a chorus, a decision would have to be made about whether she should drop the course. Or perhaps the teacher might adapt the requirements for her. If she is only partially tone-deaf, he would have to determine how far she could be expected to go with singing.

Another example of a specific dysfunction occurred in an English class. Jinny, a very intelligent girl in many ways, entered twelfth grade not only unable to spell but also unable to form many letters clearly. Because she was quite articulate, her first-semester English teacher that year was amazed at the garble of letters he saw on her virtually illegible papers. He tried to insist that she consult a dictionary about almost every word she wrote. The second-semester teacher, also unaware of Jinny's problem when she entered the class, saw that her writing was abnormal. The student told him she'd never been able to write. Notwithstanding, her wit was apparent even from the title of her first paper: "'Oh, Grow Up Plants'! Jerry Baker Raises Flowers by Talking to Them." When her teacher asked her if she recognized that her way of forming letters differed from that of other students, Jinny mentioned some diagnostic tests she had taken in second grade.

Confirming her story with her guidance counselor and with her mother, the teacher learned that those tests showed a brain dysfunction causing Jinny to transpose the normal order of letters in a word and to alter the normal shapes of some letters. The mother further explained that as reluctant as she was to accept her child's impairment, even a private therapist had been unable to help Jinny improve. The following solution was then worked out. Jinny was required to write all the papers the other students in the class did. Sometimes her sister corrected her spelling and typed her papers for her, and at other times Jinny simply read them to her teacher. Her grade was determined by how well she did in all of the tested areas of writing except spelling. Although this meant that a paper literally impossible to read could receive an A, it seemed unfair to reward or penalize her for being physically unable to spell. However, her teacher warned her about complications her disability would carry later in life. He didn't want her to think that an A in English implied she was qualified for jobs involving writing.

Jinny's case was unusual because spelling was the only conspicuous flaw of her work. When a student is having difficulty in a subject, it's frequently not so easy to pinpoint the trouble exactly. One tenth-grader, Michael, wrote as if he had never been taught any punctuation. His grammar was also nonstandard much of the time, even though he lived in a community where standard English was spoken. His spelling, while not as abnormal as Jinny's, was poor. All of these flaws aside, the content of his papers was normally solid. He always substantiated his points with clear details, something unusual for high school students, and he had a flair for figurative expression. His English teacher assumed that Michael had never bothered to learn the mechanics of the language because he had gotten by with his natural gift for content. Accordingly, for the first six weeks of school this teacher gave Michael supplementary instruction about matters he should have learned in elementary school and then held him to a tenth-grade level of performance. When he did not improve very much during the year, his teacher thought that once again he was relying on his ideas to get him through. Only by chance conversation the following summer did his teacher discover that Michael had been in "special" classes in grade school. The teacher felt somewhat as a doctor might who had prescribed spicy foods as an appetite excitant only to learn later that his patient had a past history of ulcers.

For various reasons, pertinent background information about students is not automatically given to teachers; often they have no direct access to permanent records and they have to seek out data from whatever sources they can, including the student himself, his family, and his guidance counselor. In Michael's case there were logical grounds for the teacher not to suspect any special dysfunction. No pattern to his errors was apparent. To learn grammar and punctuation requires a "good ear," which seemingly he had, as his written dialogue revealed. To learn grammar and punctuation also requires abstract thinking; his ability to reason and to write figuratively indicated that he was capable of this. Nevertheless, his teacher repeatedly reflected on the discrepancy between Michael's ideas and his mechanical expression of them. That unusualness should have been the teacher's clue to find out as much as possible about this student's ability before he determined what to hold him accountable for.

Much more numerous than cases of physical disability are those of emotional trauma, or at least cases in which psychological reasons are claimed to interfere with performance. The danger for a teacher is that he hears these pleas so often he may become immune to them. Billy can't get his work in this month because his mother died; that seems reasonable, of course. Then there's Frances, whose parents have recently divorced; naturally she's also too distraught to work. Barbara's father pressures her too much for perfection, so she rebels by not working. Sue's dog had a hysterectomy, just too threatening for a young girl. Even Great-aunt Willie's ingrown toenail is supposed to explain why John can't do his algebra.

Teachers hear stories like those fast and furiously; they hear them from students, from parents, from guidance counselors, and sometimes from administrators. In their exasperation, teachers may begin to say, "Everybody has troubles. Do your work or else." Obviously, though, a simplistic stance like that isn't a wise approach; it blinds teachers to instances in which emotional problems really do interfere with schoolwork. Moreover, teachers usually find that no one tries to explain cases of genuine suffering by pat answers like the above. There's too much that defies explanation about people who are truly sick as, for example, Connie. She did no work in any of her courses for two entire semesters. Although she expressed concern about her record, she apparently couldn't alter her behavior. In class she mostly seemed to daydream. Her teachers never knew the cause of Connie's problems, even though there were various meetings about her, with her, and with her parents. She was called a "troubled" girl, an epithet very obvious in her expression. Evidently there were numerous problems within the home. The girl herself was under the care of a private therapist, and she seemed to be receiving some form of medication from him.

Most teachers feel fortunate when administrators relieve them of the responsibility of decision in baffling cases like this one. However, many times with little specific information a teacher must decide what to do. Naturally, his response will reflect his own attitude toward emotional problems. Some of Connie's teachers, for instance, held her to the same standards as they did the rest of the class and failed her for no work. Not wishing such a devastating penalty because they felt something was truly amiss, other teachers gave her a C for no performance. Still others gave her an incomplete, hoping she would make up the work. If all of these solutions seem imperfect, be aware that there is no panacea. From a teacher's point of view it might seem logical that these youngsters would be better off if they dropped classes temporarily, but therapists frequently suggest that they remain in school so that their environment is as normal as possible. By the way, therapists may also seek out classroom teachers' observations about a student, since teachers are often with students more than any other adults except their parents.

Occasionally teachers notice symptoms of acute distress in students. Although these signs can be perplexing, they shouldn't be dismissed as insignificant. In one instance a history teacher saw that one of his students was behaving strangely. The boy was extremely fidgety, and his eyes were glazed much of the time. In talking with him privately, the teacher learned that he had grandiose schemes for himself, all in quite different areas. One moment he was talking about being a Hebrew professor—he hadn't studied any foreign languages at all—and the next an architect or a dramatist. Meanwhile his hands were shaking, and he laughed frequently, often about nothing at all. The teacher had an uneasy feeling about the boy, but since he didn't know why, he didn't say anything to anybody about his misgivings. Several weeks later the boy was discovered "fighting" a soft-drink vending machine in the student center. Not easily subdued, he was finally led to the principal's office, where his doctor and his parents decided that he should be hospitalized. As it turned out, he was institutionalized for over a year.

Such students don't come along very often, but when they do and when teachers have evidence that behavior is abnormal, they shouldn't ignore the signs. At the least they can ascertain a student's health record from his counselor or administrator. Most likely the teacher in this case couldn't have prevented the breakdown, but the actions of all concerned, including other school and medical personnel and family, might have been more efficient had they known the teacher's insights about the case.

Students Unwilling to Learn

At the opposite extreme from those students who for whatever reason can't do the work are those who are capable but won't do it. While there are various causes for students' not working, or at least not working as much as they should, most of these boys and girls share two points in common. They think they can get by without doing the assignments. They are also convinced that what they neglect won't make much difference in their lives. Imagine a boy who's fairly certain he's going to be a carpenter. He will probably never be as motivated to learn biology as a girl who wants to be a doctor. His position is not really an unreasonable one if he actually goes in the direction he imagines. If he changes his mind, though, and opts for an occupation that requires knowledge of biology, he will wish he had worked harder in high school.

Other students neglect schoolwork because they have overextended themselves with jobs or extracurricular activities. Although teachers react differently to these complications, most consider the nature of the activity and the length of time a student will be involved in it. Whether he wants an extension for his work or an exemption from it is weighed also. A student who is editor of the yearbook, for instance, may have to work nearly around the clock on that assignment for the final two weeks of production. Most teachers would allow him to make up any missed work when that is over.

Some students presume that their activities entitle them to do less schoolwork than that required of others. A boy who works at a local grocery chain from four until ten each day might complain to his teacher that he doesn't have time to do homework. That is undoubtedly true, but the questions are whether he should keep the job at all, or work fewer hours at it. Naturally, teachers can't make personal decisions for a student, but they can discuss priorities with him and make certain he understands the consequences of a decision not to study. To exempt a student from doing any part of the regular course work because he is committed to something else seems unfair to others in his class. It's a bad habit for him too; his employers won't do him similar favors and they might even be outraged if he asks for them.

Athletes are frequently unable to study very much during a sports season since they must practice for as much as three to four hours each day. Nevertheless, many schools stipulate that athletes maintain a certain grade average. Sometimes players try to make a deal with their teachers; I could scarcely believe the first request I heard for an "advance" of sorts. The student admitted that he had not earned a C for the marking period, but he wanted me to give him one anyway. He claimed that during the next term when he didn't have to practice so much, he would study enough actually to earn an A or a B. Instead of the higher grade, though, I could give him another C so that we would then be what he called "even." I just laughed at that juggling of accounts; in fact, I teased him about it in front of his classmates. I asked him why he didn't try to work out a bargain like that with the opposing team whenever our side was losing.

Every teacher also has many lazy students. (Most are lazy at one time or another!) These are people who wait for the last minute to start an assignment or study for a test. They almost always do some work, but they have no valid reason for doing as little as they do. They're not mean or unpleasant people; they just prefer not to work. At this, many of the "lazies" are quite clever.

One way to distinguish lazy students from the truly unable is that the lazy ones are always quick to exhibit a bleeding heart. It apparently amuses them to try to fool a teacher. A typical song is, "I know I can do better, but I've really had a lot on my mind. Tomorrow I'll get busy for sure." They may even try to excuse themselves because of accidents or illnesses from the distant past. One senior claimed he couldn't recognize parts of a sentence because he had missed class when this was taught in sixth grade. He neglected to mention all his other chances since then. He was trying once again to escape until his teacher told him to forget sixth grade and at least learn the essential parts of a sentence before he graduated.

Lazy students always try to finagle favors from a teacher too. "We need more time for this assignment," they say; "you're going too fast." (If a teacher has done the assignment himself, he won't have to succumb to this sophistry.) When a test is scheduled for Thursday and lazy students haven't studied enough, they beg on Thursday for an extension until Friday. After a test is returned, they're the first to ask for another test on the same material because they claim everyone in the class did poorly. Realizing near the end of a quarter or semester that their grade is low, they plead for extra-credit work. They insist they've never heard that extra credit applies to work in addition to, not instead of, regular assignments. Since lazy students generally are concerned about their grades, poor marks have a way of convincing them to work harder—sometimes.

Lazy students have a story ready for every occasion. Most of these stories are so worn that a teacher knows whenever he hears one it's more likely to be fib than fact. In a first-period class, four students were late one day. When the teacher asked for explanations, the first said that his bus had come early and he'd missed it. The second said that his mother had detained him because he had a stomach ache. The third said that he'd left home on time, but remembering he'd left his books behind, he'd returned to get them. The last student said nothing but looked crestfallen. When the teacher asked her what the matter was, she hesitated before admitting that she couldn't think of anything else to say. The others had already taken her usual excuses.

Naturally a teacher should decide what he's going to do when he hears alibis. Let's say an assignment falls due on Thursday. A lazy student is apt to ply his teacher with something like, "I did my work last night, but I went right off and left it on the kitchen table." There are several successful ways of treating these pretenses without resorting to the policy that work's due when it's due regardless. Sending a student home at once to get the assignment would be the best way, but teachers often can't do that. If they know the parents and trust their honesty, teachers can have the student bring the work the next day with a note indicating whether the work was finished on time. What I've finally settled on is to waive all penalty for lateness until the end of the school day on which an assignment is due. This gives students a little reprieve, but it also means they can't use ploys like the "kitchen table."

All of us are lazy enough to recognize the condition when we see it. Perhaps because it's a uniquely human characteristic, we tend to laugh at it as well. Sometimes teachers have a little fun by calling a student's bluff and teasing him into admitting his procrastination. Usually only a little probing is necessary to dissolve the pretense.

Peer pressure can be forceful too if a teacher knows how to manipulate it. Of course, what one student is doing is really never the proper concern of other students unless the first is trying unfairly to wheedle special favors for himself. As teachers get to know students, the teachers can usually judge the students' stories fairly accurately. When a student asks for an extension for no good reason, it often embarrasses him if his teacher discusses his request before other students who have presented their work on time. They're generally furious. And because they don't want anyone to get a privilege not extended to the entire group, they can make a rascal understand why his teacher shouldn't grant his request.

At the same time, students often know much more about each other's personal affairs than a teacher does. If there's a valid reason why a student doesn't have his work in or needs a special favor, others in the group may know it. One day a sudden and tremendous downpour occurred about fifteen minutes before the end of the period. One of my students, who always fooled away as much time in class as he could, asked permission to go home to rescue his newborn puppies. I was incredulous. "Puppies!" I exclaimed. "What next?" However, a look at the other students convinced me that he wasn't faking this time; his dogs really would have drowned if he hadn't gone home.

Parental discipline, too, often persuades a lazy student to change his habits. Teachers, though, sometimes shy away from parent conferences. Perhaps they've been confronted by an angry parent or by a parent trying to justify or excuse his child's misbehavior. Nevertheless, for every parent who won't admit his child's faults, there are many others who do. (Some are expressly happy to have a teacher confirm what they've been trying to tell a son or daughter for years.) Quite simply, they want their children to do well in school. Parents appreciate being advised of serious academic problems before report cards come out, in order to have a chance to correct them. And parents have more convincing means of encouraging work than teachers do. If George can't drive the car for a week unless he does his physics, that deprivation stings.

Another kind of student, one who at first may appear lazy, actually isn't. At least, laziness isn't his only problem. These students don't want any special favors from a teacher until, maybe, graduation time. They tend to sit quietly and resignedly, asking and apparently expecting little. Usually they offer no explanations about why they won't work. Sometimes it appears that they have been exposed to poor teaching and therefore distrust it all. Maybe some see through the hypocrisies of those around them, and while not wishing to behave similarly themselves, nevertheless don't know what to do instead. Such cases are sad, because even though these students are often bright, they seem to have no purpose or sense of direction.

These "turned off" students, as they are frequently called, may cause the adults who work with them to feel uneasy. Their impassivity implicitly challenges the validity of work and traditional values. At any rate, the students are sometimes treated as if they were explosives. Persons in charge shift them into classes where little will be required. One very bright boy who should have been in a class of superior students was moved from an average group to one for slow learners. This meant he would get through school as quietly and as quickly as possible. What the action also conveyed, though, was that nobody cared about the student. On the other hand, to have held him to his capacity would at least have shown him that others recognized and respected his ability. Moreover, it may have convinced him that there are consequences for rejecting conventional mores and values, even though one's objections may be valid.

All students, but perhaps especially unwilling ones, are helped by knowing the general requirements of a course as soon after it begins as possible. Will they have homework and how much will it count? How late can they submit work? Can they do work for extra credit? What average must they have to get a certain letter grade? How much to pass? It isn't that they want or need to know all the daily or even weekly assignments; those would be overwhelming or forgotten or both. Usually teachers don't even know all of those the first time or two they teach a course. However, within the first several days of a term, the major items of work should be projected, as well as how much each of those will be weighed in the term's grade. Students haven't been treated fairly if they can justly claim when they get their grades that they didn't realize how much they would be penalized for not doing a particular assignment or that a given test would count as much as it did.

Average Students

As much as I sometimes despise grading papers, the first several sets from any class usually do hold my interest. Reading their work is the best way I have of distinguishing my students, of seeing who can do what. Performance, of course, is all teachers measure when they label one student as average, another as below average or as superior. A student's actual capability may be quite different.

Some teachers prefer average students to those at either extreme. As people, average students tend to be less complicated. However, it is also difficult to help average students stay motivated for academic work. Their past school record alone often convinces them that there's little they can do to improve. As one of the wittiest students I've ever taught retorted when I asked him why he didn't work more: "You give me C's. I've always gotten them. There'll be a C on my tombstone."

Although motivation and innate ability always figure strongly in performance, teachers can do only a limited amount about the former and they can do nothing about the latter. What they really have to be concerned about is the other variable in performance—that is, the manner of instruction itself. Ironically, a classroom teacher sometimes has to remind himself that he doesn't teach classes. He doesn't teach individuals either. He teaches individuals in classes. He must find a balance between group instruction and personal instruction, must realize when the first suffices and when the second is essential. Group instruction is enhanced when a teacher can anticipate typical kinds of problems that students are likely to have with his particular subject. That information, which comes primarily from experience in teaching a subject, allows a teacher to remove inevitable stumbling blocks students will face. One doesn't need to have taught at all, though, to understand generally why students who are at least partially willing and able might nevertheless have more difficulty than they should in learning. Those reasons are basically three: students may fail to understand a teacher's instruction; they may be unable to apply it; or they may become discouraged as they try to carry it out. Merely isolating one of these causes in a given instance helps a teacher understand better how to help students improve.

The fault doesn't invariably lie with the students. When they don't seem to learn, a teacher should consider first whether his explanation was clear. He may have thought they knew more about the subject than they did. As discussed previously, that assumption baffles an audience. He may have given them more information than they could grasp at one time. Students need time not only to listen but also to write down what they hear. The teacher may have failed to define the goal of the work specifically enough. Although nothing in education courses is stressed more than outlining clear objectives, once the teacher has projected general goals, he sometimes forgets that students want to know what they're supposed to learn on a daily basis. Finally, the teacher himself may not have been entirely certain about a given point and he may have tried to cover up his uncertainty with words. Any of these situations confuses students. They may not care or know enough to ask a question, but they won't learn much either.

Often a problem in understanding arises because a teacher means one thing by a word, whereas to students that term means something altogether different. Suppose a history teacher assigns students to investigate a specific topic in twentieth-century European history. World War I will seem very specific to a student who has been accustomed in junior high to researching his reports almost solely in encyclopedias. He may feel that there wouldn't be enough information for him to write a paper about a more limited topic on that subject. Even the encyclopedia devotes only a few pages to World War I. How could he write more than that? If his teacher asks him what part of World War I he will write about, the student will probably think the causes of that war would be a severely restricted topic. He can't imagine that the causes of a particular battle are really more what his teacher had in mind.

To help a student like this adequately, a teacher himself usually has to suggest a suitable topic. This is not doing a student's work for him either. Whether he's in high school or graduate school, he won't be able to write a good paper without a good topic. And he can't learn how to write a good paper by writing a poor one. All he learns from the latter is that academic work is frustrating.

It's often said that when we look at something we see only what we want to see. The principle applies equally to listening. A person's conception of what he should be hearing can cause him to block out or to distort what he actually hears. For instance, in any skill involving speed, a student's natural tendency is to want to go fast. Say a violinist in an orchestra is racing along with a selection he is practicing but is still missing notes. His teacher will tell him that speed is unimportant at first, that speed follows perfection while the reverse is impossible. A student, though, imagines that speed must be important. Would Isaac Stern be a virtuoso if he played all of his pieces at a snail's pace? No student could believe that someone as talented as that artist must play slowly as he learns a number. A student violinist may not truly "hear" what his teacher says about the relationship between speed and correctness until long after he has graduated, if then. In the meanwhile, the only way he will be able to improve is if his teacher prescribes a tempo at which he can play all the notes of a selection correctly. That distance between principle and application of principle is why pragmatic teachers sometimes resort to an approach that might be summarized as, "Don't worry about why, just do."

Many students can't or won't "do," though, unless a teacher first convinces them that what he is saying is correct. When students resist a teacher's instructions, they frequently conclude that he just doesn't appreciate the quality of their work. They feel that his criticisms are picayune and that they can't do what "that teacher wants." This was the case with one composition student; her own notions of good writing prevented her from understanding what the teacher tried to convey. To this student good writing meant flowery expressions and uncommon words: she believed these were literary. Perhaps by the time she had struggled through a sentence she thought she knew what it meant and therefore her readers should too. Imagine trying to decipher this one: "The Bear was the canal that led Shakespeare's stream of nature consciousness." Correcting a style of this sort involves re-education in taste, a slow and often painful undertaking. From her reading the girl had picked up something of the rhythm and vocabulary of professional writers. She didn't quite realize that there is more to writing than rhythm and high-sounding words. One thing that startled her was to read her teacher's comments about her papers, comments attempted in the same gobbledygook as hers.

Forcing a student like this to acknowledge her problem is only a part of the process. She can't improve until she learns specifically how to go about changing. Frequently students understand what a teacher says, but unless they also have a technique to apply the instruction, they won't succeed. This becomes very apparent when one is teaching any motor skill. Suppose a physical-education student is trying to learn golf. Although she has listened carefully to her teacher's instructions to the class, her shots persistently veer off to the right instead of going straight. Her teacher tells her that what she must do is to "break" her wrists or turn them up as far as she can at the top of her swing. Simple! Not to her. Initially she can't make that movement unless her teacher holds on to one end of her club, thus forcing her wrists into the proper position.

What she must do is train her muscles. If she becomes a good golfer, she won't think about her swing; her muscles will do that for her. Her teacher could hit the ball beautifully even with his eyes closed. As one learns any motor skill, the muscles don't know what they are supposed to do. The technique is to perform the same movement repeatedly until they learn it. The more complicated a movement, the longer it may take a student to be able to do what he understands he should be doing and what he wants to do. (Incidentally, in cases like these, instructions would be facilitated if teachers could show students physically as well as tell them what to do. Because high school students sometimes misinterpret such "intimacy," most teachers rely on models or pictures for demonstration.)

A common type of instruction that students can't apply is that involving reading. Of course, most high school students believe they can read. A teacher assigns the first chapter and the students go off and read it. Often, though, they come back the next day reporting that while they read every word they can't remember anything they read. I personally am always sympathetic when I hear that plea because I remember myself propped in front of numerous books in a university library. As much as I wanted to learn the material, I couldn't keep my mind on what I was reading. I thought I was to blame. Books were more or less sacred, and anyway I didn't think a teacher would have us read anything but the best books.

My shock was no small one when it came. All teachers realize that some of the reading they assign is dull. Often they have no choice; no better text exists. Moreover, even masterpieces usually have parts that are ponderous. If teachers are candid with students about this, all the teachers accomplish is to make students feel that the material they read is insignificant. However, without commenting on quality, a teacher can guide students in what to read for in an assignment. This "handle" to the material gives them a way to distinguish major ideas from minor ones. It's rare that a person remembers nothing of what he has read; more often various ideas are simply jumbled in his mind. If he is to grasp the contents of a chapter or a book, he has to organize its information; the teacher's pointers can help him do that.

Most high school students haven't really been instructed in the assimilation of large amounts of written material. They're likely to think that reading by itself means learning. Sometimes as students discuss a work in class one will say something like, "Oh, I thought about that as I was reading but didn't believe it would be important." Convincing a student to follow those hunches instead of suppressing them shows him how to "converse" with a book. It doesn't matter whether he asks so-called significant questions or trivial ones. The important thing is that he is actively thinking about the words he is reading rather than merely allowing them to pass before his eyes. In this way he can begin to appreciate how any book can be made to yield its meaning.

Most students also don't realize that writing down what they have read helps them to learn it. Even eager students complain about having to summarize a chapter, an assignment they insist is babyish. They don't see that careful analysis of any material rests on careful summary. What they really don't like is having to clarify their thinking. If they have persuaded themselves they know something, they don't like being forced to acknowledge whether or not they actually do. Of course, a written summary is valuable, too, as a later reminder of what one has read, but many students haven't taken enough comprehensive examinations to see a need for that.

Although there's a difference between knowing a subject and good performance on an exam, many times students feel that they knew more than they were able to show on a test. Sometimes that reflects carelessness in taking a test; as often it suggests that they haven't been shown how to study for a test or how to approach various types of exam questions. First, most students do not distinguish review from intensive study. They don't know that intensive study isn't simply reading of previously read material. They can be taught to concentrate on what they need to learn about the material, to ask and answer questions about it, and to solve problems.

Second, students should be encouraged to practice taking tests. Like any other skill, the ability to take tests well must be developed, and one cannot do that in testing sessions alone. The need to practice almost always seems more apparent to students in subjects that center around problem solving, but the technique applies equally to other subjects. When I was a freshman in college, our art history professor had us prepare for the midyear exam by making up and writing out the answers for six essay questions. We asked her if she was telling us to second-guess her. She replied that although we'd never be able to do that, we'd benefit by practice and we'd be surprised at how much of our answers we could use for the questions she would compose.

Teachers can also help students if teachers show them that various types of exam questions presume particular approaches. In multiple-choice questions, for instance, most students read the entire statement from beginning to end. Naturally it makes no sense. They should be instructed to convert a multiple-choice question into multiple true-false statements by reading the common heading with each choice separately. Students think that they don't have to be as precise on essay questions as they do with objective ones, but that sense of freedom leads many of them astray. They simply start to write without reading the question carefully and without planning the points they will cover, as well as the support for those points. It's not very difficult for them to learn that when they tackle an essay test that way, they're likely to ramble or to be unable to complete their answers.

Lack of technique or faulty technique hinders many students from following a teacher's instructions. The students' difficulty is increased if they give in to the natural tendency to be uncritical about what they have done. Although personal objectivity is never easy to muster, a lack of it becomes bothersome when a technique needs change. If a faulty technique becomes ingrained, a person can literally be blind to what would be immediately apparent to anyone else. One boy's papers were inevitably criticized for their wordiness, but he couldn't appreciate the justice of that. He even argued at first that there was no repetitiveness in the following excerpt: "The experience of working with an accountant who knows his business will profit me greatly. This will surely help me also. I know I will be a better accountant because of it." He didn't really understand what was amiss until his teacher worked with him personally on several of his papers. Interestingly, when the class did exercises on brevity, he could work those well. What he couldn't establish was a connection between those and his own work. And although he was embarrassed when he finally began to understand what his teacher had been trying to tell him, that didn't mean he was never guilty of another redundancy. His teacher helped him to become more conscious of the practice by requiring him to condense and revise all paragraphs in which repetitions occurred. When breaking a habit is necessary to advance, though, discouragement is inevitable.

At other times students lack confidence because they look only at the end results they want, and they fear they will never be able to accomplish those. A teacher shouldn't argue with such a real fear; students usually can't perform the task when they start even though they may be capable of it. A teacher's best recourse is to prove the fear false. Say a football coach wants his team to do fifty pushups a day by opening game three weeks away. That number will probably startle his players if they can do only ten a day when he announces it. If they can do ten, though, they can also do fifty if the coach increases the number slightly each day. Known as approximation, this method of gradual increments is effective with all kinds of subjects. People fear quantity because they think a task will get harder as it gets bigger. Sometimes it does, but it doesn't necessarily have to.

Students also become discouraged when they don't progress as quickly as they think they should. In most skills a person does not make discernible progress on a daily or even a weekly basis. Maybe it takes months before he all of a sudden can do something better. Although that new plateau would have been impossible had he not practiced the skill continually, to practice for a long time without improving is disheartening. This situation occurs in almost any kind of learning. Insight comes in a flash, but preparation that makes the insight possible is usually arduous. During the struggle a teacher's confidence may be the main incentive a student has to continue to work.

Any student, regardless of his ability and motivation, benefits from a teacher's encouragement. A student also benefits from a teacher's patience. When a student is having difficulty with a subject, sometimes he needs a teacher's patience almost more than anything else. Patience, though, is not an easy trait for a teacher to acquire. His job almost works against it since he must explain the same processes and facts, year in, year out. There probably isn't a teacher alive who hasn't occasionally felt like saying to a student, "But I've already explained that to you two or three times. What's the matter with you?" Actually, a teacher might better ask that question of himself unless the rebuke was prompted by a student's inattentiveness. Teaching students is really somewhat analogous to a robin teaching her young to fly. Two or three chirps are not enough. Over and over again the robin calls, no change detectable in her notes, until each fledgling ventures—first, a number of long hops, and then a daring ascent.

Superior Students

Fortune appears to smile on some people. Intelligent and talented, they know how to use these gifts to their advantage. Throughout their school years, they are often outstanding academically, athletically, and socially, and after they graduate many remain distinguished. I wonder, though, how lucky they think they are. Because they are more capable than others, more is required of them. Even as young children, many have had to show off their talents for eager and approving parents and teachers. If not compelled by others to achieve, these students drive themselves.

Recognizing such youngsters is never difficult. Their vocabulary and their questions are more sophisticated than those of average learners. Sometimes superior students embarrass a teacher because they notice details about the work that he hadn't thought of. Although the idea that gifted students can learn without working is untrue, often the time they require is less than that needed by average students. Normally gifted students excel in all their subjects, so much so that townspeople may complain about a school's favoring the same students all the time. It often happens, though, that the best mathematicians and chemists in a school will also be the most talented writers and artists.

Bright students are not invariably sought after by all teachers. Perhaps they instinctively fear trying to teach anyone more intelligent and capable than they. Then, too, gifted students can be obnoxious. Granted their ability is something to be proud of, but pride turned to conceit is never appealing, and conceit coupled with condescension toward others becomes almost unbearable. A superior group whose leaders are arrogant is not a very enjoyable one to teach. Furthermore, gifted students can be quite argumentative. Suppose one announces before his classmates that there's no point to the method the teacher has told them to use. The gifted student claims that his own shortcut is just as good. Or another student may state categorically that there's no value in a particular book they've been asked to read. The relative justice of their complaints aside, these students can very cleverly debate the validity of their ideas. If a teacher isn't careful, he might appear foolish.

So what's wrong, some might insist, with a teacher appearing foolish from time to time? Shouldn't students, especially gifted ones, learn that everyone makes mistakes? I suspect, however, that most high school students, especially gifted ones, have long since learned that everyone errs, and there's also a big difference between saying that everybody makes mistakes and implying that everybody *ought* to. I once bet a boy in a bright class a batch of brownies that Ingmar Bergman had directed a particular film. In fact, Bergman had not, and the boy knew the actual director. The class was amused and they enjoyed my cakes, but could they have thought much of me for being so stupid?

Not long ago I was teaching Faulkner's *Go Down Moses,* and a student questioned one of my points. On the spot and given that abstruse novel, I couldn't decide whether the girl was right or not. However, after study that night convinced me she was, I began class the next day by thanking her for her correction. When people say that students respect a teacher who can admit he's wrong, most likely what they really mean is that students would despise one who tried to cover up an error they recognized.

Sometimes it is suggested that bright students learn more when a teacher drops his pedagogical cloak. In other words, instead of being a "teacher" instructing "students," he is just a person learning along with other people. Students will be motivated to learn because they will feel important. The problem with that notion is that the teacher's stance can be only a pose. And students will quickly recognize this. A teacher and students should not be equally informed about the material of a course. If the teacher actually knows no more than the students, there's no reason for them to study with him.

Like all students, talented ones need direction in what to learn. If they are studying history, for example, they will know little more initially than less capable students about prominent persons, events, and ideas of any age. Nor will they know how to find the best sources for learning about an age. Interestingly, they are often unadept at comprehending human motivation. Perhaps they have not lived long enough, but it may be that they will always have difficulty in understanding why most people think and act as they do. On the other hand, with little help from their teacher they may see various ramifications of events and ideas, and most gifted students have accurate recall of what they read and discuss.

Superior students also need teachers to provide a disciplined structure for study, even though they may resist that structure. For instance, some will complain about having a particular number of problems to work each night or so many pages to read. They say that's too much like grade school, where the teacher told them exactly when to do what. It appears, though, that left to themselves, most people would not educate themselves beyond those skills necessary to survive or thrive in a society. Can we expect many Benjamin Franklins, Abraham Lincolns, or Eric Hoffers? Sometimes bright students even ask a teacher to assign certain books the students regard as difficult but important. They know they do not really have the incentive and discipline to read them on their own.

Generally speaking, superior students are extremely grade-conscious. They have to be to fulfill their ambitions for colleges and professions. Their academic history also fosters the trait. A student who's usually received C's won't complain to a teacher about receiving another; he expects that grade. Nor will a C student be as likely to argue about a D as an A student will be to dispute a B. One ambitious girl asked me near the end of a year why she had gotten only one A+ on a paper. She said she couldn't help being peeved with herself for A's and A−'s. (I suspect she was peeved with me even more than with herself.) Quite simply, though, while these students are diligent, they do not automatically do as well as they might in every course they take. As with other students, their motivation partly stems from their enjoyment of a subject and partly from their conception of its usefulness. Since they do well, however, most teachers don't have time or energy to fret much about these A−'s or B's.

Although no other teaching may be as demanding, none is more enjoyable than teaching a capable and successful student who is also an amiable person. He usually has more wit than an average student; he is also interested in more topics. A roomful of such persons will often make the subject lively even if the teacher doesn't. They assume the importance of books and ideas much more readily than average learners, and they want, sometimes almost desperately, to discuss the practicality of the ideas they hear and read about.

A social studies class was discussing Benjamin Franklin as the prototype of the American Dream. The drift of most of the discussion, which could only have occurred in an affluent community, was that material goods don't bring happiness and may bring spiritual decay. A girl in the group finally objected that she knew a great many people who enjoyed their possessions and she didn't see why that was wrong. She held up the pencil on her desk and asked, "If working for pencils makes me happy, why shouldn't I do it?" Regardless of what she finally decided to do, she probably will never forget the answer of one of her classmates: "What good is a pencil if you have nothing to write?"

Among superior students occasionally there are persons of truly exceptional talent. Ironically, teachers may be unable to recognize their very best students, at least while they're teaching them. That's one reason why so many geniuses don't do very well in school. Every teacher has a standard by which he imagines and measures greatness. When a student deviates from that standard, whether below it or above it, his teacher will not consider him as talented as other students.

I have taught many talented youngsters, who will surely become prominent actors, politicians, teachers, businessmen, or whatever. One student, though, outranked all of these; he seemed to have a kind of genius for writing fiction. It was not so much that his stories were written fluently because many students can do that. It was that they captured emotions truthfully. When I read his work, I remembered what it was like to be a child or a teen-ager. His dialogue was also beautifully true to life. Writing fiction was not required in the course this boy was taking, but early that fall he started bringing his stories to me. What surprised me was that even though he was basically a shy person, he almost forced his work on me at first. I really could not teach him much about writing stories. We edited his work carefully, and I showed him how other writers have solved particular technical problems. However, what he wanted from me was not instruction as much as hearing the delight I took in his work. My praise seemed to keep him going. Interestingly, when I first met him, he appeared an unlikely candidate for my "most talented student" award. In a class of average learners, he didn't read much, something that always makes anyone suspect in an English teacher's eyes. Also his essays about the literature we studied were not at all exceptional. Until well past the midpoint of the year, he seemed a perfectly average student—except for his stories.

Is anybody ever "perfectly average"? As convenient as typing students may be, the danger of this approach is that no student ever comes neatly packaged ready to fit into a mold precisely. Furthermore, there is much overlapping of ability groups. Students with limited capacities or with specific dysfunctions may be motivated enough to accomplish as much as students with a great deal more talent. Conversely, bright students are often lazy or unmotivated. Then, too, personal growth and crises, as well as the manner of instruction itself, may cause a student to shift from one to another of the categories within any year.

For these reasons it is impossible to predict exactly what a student will or will not be able to do. But after a few years in the classroom, it is very easy for teachers to presume that they know how much ability or drive is needed for a given occupation and to imagine they can invariably recognize these characteristics when they see them. Teachers may say something like, "That person will never make a doctor; he just doesn't have what it takes." How do they know whether he does? Maybe he just hasn't shown them.

A classic error in judgment involved twins. During their senior year in high school, both boys wanted to apply to universities to pursue studies in liberal arts. Their parents were advised by school personnel that some form of technical training would be more appropriate since neither seemed talented enough to graduate from college. When one of the sons objected that both he and his brother had scored far above average on their SAT's, school personnel countered that the boys merely knew "how to take tests." Happily, the parents listened to their sons rather than to teachers and guidance counselors. Both boys subsequently earned advanced degrees from well-known universities; one is now a university professor himself, the other a translator and critic.

We still know very little about what actually occurs in the brain when people learn. Moreover, teachers cannot possibly be aware of all of the many factors that contribute to their students' motivation to learn. Is it really the function of teachers ever to discourage a student from attempting something he wants to do? If he can't do it, he'll discover that soon enough for himself. He certainly won't thank anybody for advance information about his shortcomings.

When asked whether he knows how to do any specific task, whatever it is, a friend of mine usually replies, "Maybe I do; I haven't tried." Most people smile at his whimsy, which they do not regard as a very realistic appraisal of ability. Perhaps, though, students would benefit if teachers could be just this optimistic. Teachers would not be requiring anyone to do what he can't. They would not be forcing anyone to do what he really doesn't wish. Rather they would be trying to extend a student's possibilities. After all, maybe he can!

IV
Student Behavior in the Classroom

Of all the aspects of teaching, maintaining an orderly classroom often seems initially the most difficult. Before a teacher knows what has happened, students are talking and laughing when they're supposed to be listening or working. They yell, throw things around the room, lean out the window, and do about anything else that strikes their fancy. When their teacher tells them to stop such nonsense, they just laugh or otherwise disregard him.

The amazing thing is, however, that most teachers who remain in the profession over a year or two learn to avoid that kind of chaos. This is partly because there's so little enjoyment in their work when classes are disorderly. It is also because teachers are literally forced to become knowledgeable about the desirable and the undesirable ways human beings act when they are in groups. Besides this, teachers learn to anticipate differences in each class, although common problems are likely to occur. These problems run the gamut from mischief to immoral and illegal behavior. In between these extremes are disruptions stemming from the way a teacher and students interact and the way students get along with each other.

Moreover, teachers come to see that it's not just students who must act a certain way in the classroom. A teacher himself must be willing and able to insist that students behave themselves. One colleague of mine used to jest that she would be far better equipped to deal with student misconduct if she could carry her shotgun to class. As appalling as that might sound, it does figuratively suggest what a teacher has to do. While he shouldn't be easily provoked, he mustn't hesitate to discipline students when necessary. They must understand that he is unwavering about their conforming to the recognized standard of acceptable classroom behavior.

Pranks: Their Influence on Class Character

Some classes in any school are known for inventive pranks; other classes are devoid of them. Whether they occur depends mainly on student interaction with their leaders. Since these disruptions can help a group to become more cohesive and friendly, no one really expects a teacher to do much about them. Actually, teachers who are absolutely intolerant of mischief unwittingly incite it. Most teachers prefer to let students enjoy the feeling that they've gotten away with something, provided the interruption isn't long and no real harm is done. Anyway, I think most teachers like such jokes as much as students, even though the teachers don't necessarily let them know that.

No trick is favored more by students than trying to get teachers off the subject of the lesson. Ways of achieving this are devious too. One greatly used tactic is a student question about the teacher's favorite topic. I remember how we conspired against our Latin teacher when I was in high school. She would frequently delay the lesson when a student asked about a current issue at our school, be it new uniforms for the band, the senior class trip, or the Board of Education's objection to the latest editorial in the student newspaper. Each day before class we plotted who would ask the first question, as well as which ones to have in reserve in case the discussion of the first didn't last long enough. I laugh now when I recall how we thought we fooled her. However, she wasn't for a minute hoodwinked by us. Even though we could never have imagined it then, maybe some days she didn't want to work any more than we did, and our questions gave her the excuse she needed to dally. Moreover, she obviously thought there were important matters to be learned other than Latin conjugations and declensions. We were not, though, allowed to have such discussions every day. She realized when issues extraneous to the lesson should be terminated.

Students not only like to get off the subject, they also like to get "out of" the subject, and they are ingenious inventors of reasons to do so. One student must consult with his guidance counselor briefly; another has to make an urgent phone call; another picked up by mistake the wrong book from his locker. Variations of these ploys are endless. Sometimes a friend knocks on the door and calls a student out. A favorite gambit is for two or three of them to arrange to be out of the room at the same time. In one instance a girl slid from her seat to the floor and seemed to pass out. In the confusion of the moment, the teacher's only concern was to help her, and he quickly covered her with his jacket. When she opened her eyes a few seconds later, several of her pals volunteered to accompany her to the nurse. The teacher suspected something was foul after they had left because the rest of the class was atwitter but not with the kind of surprised excitement that normally accompanies a genuine crisis. Even though they soon settled back to work, it happened that they had all been in on the joke, as the teacher later discovered. The girls knew that they could get away with their stunt. Since teachers don't decide matters of health, they can't hesitate to send a patient, real or feigned, to a nurse. And no nurse will be reluctant to let a student rest all period, even though the nurse in this case later concurred with the teacher's doubts about the genuineness of this "illness."

When I first started to teach, I used to wonder why my classes differed so much. Variations were apparent even when I taught two or more sections of the same course. The "atmosphere" in the classes was never quite the same; each group seemed to possess what might be called its own personality. This occurred even though I prepared for the classes in the same way and the students in the sections had generally the same ability. In one instance the section of a course that met the last period in the afternoon usually caused me to wonder what possibly could happen next, whereas the other section couldn't have been duller.

One day I mentioned in the afternoon section that I thought our classroom looked a little shabby. The students agreed and we decided we'd try to spruce it up. We didn't have time that day, though, to make our plans. The next day the student leader and the class clown were five minutes late to class. When they appeared they came rushing in with a six-foot artificial marlin. As they mounted our first "decoration" in the front of the room, the class exploded in laughter. I suppose it was the surprise, coupled with the incongruity of seeing a mounted marlin in an English class, at least a class that wasn't studying Melville or Hemingway. Because of such antics, though, that class had more happy youngsters in it than almost any I've ever taught. The reason was simple, too: the leader and the clown, close personal friends, refused to let a class become dull. If they were a little zanier at times than I usually prefer students to be, I knew they would seldom allow their classmates to become bored.

Had they stopped with jokes, they might have kept us entertained, but they wouldn't have contributed much to making a good class. Importantly, even though the clown often tried to appear flippant, both he and the leader were interested in the work of the course. Their questions would frequently touch off a round of queries by other students. Moreover, their questions were the type that any teacher likes because these boys unhesitatingly asked whatever they didn't understand about the work—points, ironically, that students' pride often prevents them from raising.

On the other hand, the section of the course that met first period had no such dominating personalities to help the students enjoy themselves and at the same time to keep them interested in the subject. These students never misbehaved; I almost wished at times they would since that at least would have brought some life into the class. Their stupor could not be blamed on lack of intelligence either, as their tests and papers revealed. There was simply no enthusiasm about work or about anything else. The student leader, who happened also to be the most outspoken person in the class, had little use for school academically or socially, and she disdained anyone who felt differently. She frequently arrived late, groaned no matter what the assignment, and sighed and rolled her eyes when any student tried to question or comment on the subject. This obvious distaste for school, shared by the girl's friends, set them apart from the other, more sober group of students in the class, who were already geared toward professional careers. Their differences were even marked physically by the very clothes they wore: black tee-shirts with embroidered red lips, for example, as opposed to muted pastel blouses. It may have been that the more conservative students were envious of those in the opposite faction, who were somewhat more independent than they. The students in these two groups seldom spoke to each other; however, their expressions bespoke the increasing contempt they felt as the year wore on. Since nothing I tried to do to help them relax and forget about themselves seemed to work, the end result was a class that was spiritless and often wearying to us all.

Examples like these finally forced me to think clearly about the character of classes. It is true that a class is affected by the time it meets. Most people are less lively at eight in the morning than they are at two. It is also true that the temperament of a class is somewhat dependent upon the way students in a room react to the personality of the teacher and, for that matter, to the way the teacher reacts to the students. The above examples imply that I was amused by the class clown, while I was put on the defensive by the leader in the other class. Nevertheless, equal to the importance of these factors is the way the students get along with each other; their relationship is usually influenced by the personality of the class leader.

A group, by the way, is never responsible for serious trouble. While a number of students might become involved in an incident, it is usually one, or less often two or three, who are the instigators. Many times the actual leader takes no apparent role in the misbehavior; he just sits back and watches others do his bidding. This is why teachers are advised to be aware of leaders in their classes and to be wary of alienating them. What nobody ever bothers explaining, though, is how a teacher is supposed to recognize a leader.

Characteristics of Leaders

In uncomplicated situations a bold student may simply and openly take charge of student affairs. Once two classmates were injured in a car accident on the evening of the third day of school. The next day another boy asked me if he could have a few moments of class time to tell the others what had happened. With no difficulty whatsoever, he convinced that entire class, including those who did not know the injured students at all, to contribute fifty cents each for the purchase of flowers and a card. He then appointed persons to buy those items, although he himself supervised the signing of the card in class the next day. While his motivation appeared entirely unselfish, his move clinched his authority for the rest of the year. He had directed the class in something that made them feel good, and he had also shown that he knew when to delegate responsibility and when to act himself.

Leadership, however, is not always dependent on friendly cooperation. In maintaining their authority, some student leaders are not at all hesitant about using force. Their tactics might be compared to those of the kingpin squirrel who has come to "own" the birdfeeder in my backyard. It's easy to see why that squirrel can frighten the birds away. But how is he able to keep two other squirrels approximately his own size from feeding at "his" station? He does it because he's in charge there, and he's in charge because of his physical aggressiveness. Whenever the other two approach the feeder, he chases them off at once. They run too. After he sets matters aright, I'm always tickled to see him climb to the top of the feeder, flick his tail, and look for all the world like some lord inspecting his dominion.

Student leaders, of course, don't have to rely solely on their classmates' fear of physical aggression. The threat of social ostracism is also a powerful weapon, as was demonstrated in one class when a holiday get-together was announced. The teacher assumed it would be impossible for everyone to attend the party, since it was scheduled for a time outside the normal school hours. For some reason she never entirely understood, though, the boy who originated the idea for the affair wanted 100 percent attendance. One of his classmates balked and told him after class that he didn't want to go because he didn't think he would have much fun. The leader, beyond what he thought was his teacher's earshot, snapped back at him, "You'd better show up." Towering over that leader by at least a head, the boy who had raised the objection nevertheless smiled meekly in response; he went to the party. As the teacher later found out, he was afraid that if he didn't go, the leader would exclude him from his personal group of buddies.

Another and one of the best means teachers have of discovering students with leadership capacity is providing opportunities for that ability to be demonstrated. A teacher often needs student assistance. Perhaps materials must be distributed or a room readied for the showing of a film. If volunteers are sought to direct and supervise these activities, not merely to follow the teacher's directives, it is usually a leader who will want to take charge.

Some leaders, though, both good and bad ones, have reasons for wishing to remain anonymous to the teacher. That's all right as long as things go smoothly. Anyway, not all discipline problems are incited by a leader. Incidents prompted by individual problems occur frequently and are dealt with best by direct personal consultation with the individual. However, if trouble arises and a number of students are involved, the teacher has to discover who the instigator is without confronting the group with that question. The teacher can then apply the process of elimination to narrow the possibilities of who is behind it. Which student would take charge, the teacher has to decide, if this class were left without adult supervision?

The most obvious characteristic of a leader is that he must want or at least be willing to direct others. Leaders are convinced that without direction other people won't know what to do; things will run amuck. A leader I know said once that while she didn't really want to boss, "somebody has to." Naturally, that kind of confidence and assertiveness would be unheard of in students who are at all timid. Also, any out-and-out loners would be uninterested in leadership even if they were capable of it.

A leader not only must be willing to take charge, but must also be able to persuade others to follow his leadership, through either fear or respect or both. He must always know or at least appear to know what he is doing; for this reason any mistakes must usually be camouflaged carefully. However, since nobody can be perfect, a leader knows that once in a while it's wise to admit an inconsequential error. One of the strongest leaders I have known personally exercised her sway mainly in her own family. I laughed once in disbelief when this shrewd woman began an anecdote about the "only" mistake she had made in raising her children. Even though she stopped her story long enough to acknowledge my incredulity, she did not essentially change her stance. She admitted that while she might have made additional blunders, she was unaware of them. Any students, then, given to public doubt about themselves or their plans are not leaders. This often includes some of the most intelligent persons in a class, persons whose very understanding prevents their fully supporting any kind of decisive action. They can see inherent shortcomings in virtually everything.

Sometimes an intellectual, who may or may not be truly intelligent, dominates the class discussion. Such a person, though, is usually unable to lead a group even if he has leadership ability. Americans have always been and still are a little suspicious of anyone unabashedly intellectual. We are more likely to respect a so-called regular person, one who is shrewd but not bookish. Actually a student who differs from the majority of the group in any way they do not respect will be unable to lead. Some classes in fact have no single strong leader, while others have a number of students capable of leadership.

A teacher must be able to spot a class leader because the only efficient way to minimize behavioral problems involving a number of students in a class is to get the cooperation of the leader. Problems usually won't end unless the student leader says they should, and he or she may not be convinced to do this unless the teacher threatens or inflicts discipline the leader personally wants to avoid.

Problems of Student/Teacher Interaction

Often there is a fine line between a group having fun and really testing a teacher. Most of a class may think that a jest is innocent when all the time their leader knows differently. Once an entire class was fifteen minutes late. When their teacher announced that they would have to make up that time after school, they pleaded for leniency, noting their otherwise good behavior. The teacher stood firm, though, because he was legally responsible for them while they had been roaming who knows where. Moreover, it sounded too much like a test to be ignored. Many youngsters in that particular group would never have cut class unless someone had put them up to it. Still, the teacher was glad that he did not have to single out the leader for punishment.

In some way every teacher will be tested by his students, especially in the beginning of his career. The subject of the test is the control of the group. If a teacher doesn't show that he can get the class to do what it should, the student leader will step in and direct matters as he or she likes. Ironically, the test is often over before a teacher knows it has begun. One new teacher wasn't satisfied with the behavior in her ninth-period algebra class. Of course, she had reprimanded the students time after time, but their conduct seemed to get worse rather than better. She didn't know why. One Friday afternoon in October a veritable war of spitballs began. Before she knew it, they were flying everywhere, and the students were noisy and unruly. She issued an ultimatum: the next person to throw a spitball would be permanently removed from the class. After that pronouncement, they settled down, and no more paper was thrown that day. On Monday, though, the leader was ready to meet her challenge. He stood up when he thought her back was turned and hurled the first missile, already nicely soaked in his mouth. Immediately that boy was ordered to go to the principal, who decided to remove him from the class. For the rest of the year, the group gave very little trouble.

This teacher was lucky—usually ultimatums mean more problems unless one can make good on them. First of all, the teacher saw who threw the spitball. Often a teacher really doesn't know who the exact culprit is. If the teacher ignores the spitball, the class wins a round. If he guesses who threw it and guesses incorrectly, the class wins by an even bigger margin. Not only does the teacher not know what's going on, but students realize he'll eventually have to back down. If he doesn't and if he punishes someone who is innocent, the entire class will rightly turn against him. The teacher was also fortunate because she was supported by her administration. Suppose the principal had said instead that the boy should be given one more chance. Where is her threat then when the leader waltzes back into the room, confident that he, not the teacher, will control the class?

As was indicated, these tests are given so quickly that teachers don't have time to think at the moment about what they're doing; they just have to act. This is why so many inexperienced teachers fail the tests. Since they haven't encountered such situations before, they don't know the best way to respond. Consider the following incident. Toward the end of a class while the teacher was assigning homework, one boy suddenly bounced a tennis ball. The teacher told him to put the ball away and he did— temporarily. Within a few seconds, though, he bounced the ball again. This time the teacher instructed him to bring her the ball. He passed it instead to the boy next to him. The teacher then told the first boy to wait outside the room and meet her when the class was over. Before the teacher barely resumed her instructions to the class, the boy who was given the ball bounced it. Now visibly shaken a little, the teacher told him also to wait outside. The ball was left on the chair the boy vacated. Once more into her directions, the teacher noticed that still a third boy had picked up the ball and was rolling it on the top of his desk. Saved by the bell! As the students were passing out of the room, the teacher asked the last boy who had picked up the ball to give it to her; instead he handed it to his friend, who, in turn, pocketed it. This simple little game had mushroomed so that within five minutes four boys were involved. Because another class was soon starting, the teacher had to tell all the boys to report after school. She then had to begin another class somewhat unnerved by the entire incident.

After school only one of the four boys appeared. He got off with a reprimand. The next day in class all was quiet; the teacher warned the other three to report after school that day or they would be reported to the principal. Eventually that had to happen. Numbers are always on the students' side; it's more difficult to insist that three rather than one do something. Students know this and they probably also understand that a teacher doesn't like to go to superiors for help, especially about a number of students, because it appears that the teacher doesn't know what he's doing.

In retrospect the teacher discovered a much simpler solution, one that could be applied to many situations. Had the teacher herself removed the temptation of the ball, at least three of the four boys would not have become implicated and maybe even the first could have been dismissed with a warning. When the teacher asked the first student to bring her the ball, she asked him to stand up before all of his peers and submit to her wish. That's a loss of face for him. With no trouble she could have gone to him for the ball and most likely have gotten it. Unless a student thinks that a teacher is very weak or unless the student is especially brazen, he will not try to snatch the ball from her hands when she takes it off his desk.

When I began teaching almost two decades ago, one of my classes was totally out of control by Thanksgiving—out of my control, anyway. Confusion reigned. I didn't become totally discouraged because my other groups were reasonably cooperative, but that class kept me modest. One March day those urchins made me so miserable that I left the room crying. They didn't kick me out of class permanently, though. To the surprise of my students, I was back with them the next day and for the rest of the year. A teacher can usually survive these dilemmas, regardless of how uncomfortable they make him, if he acts on Woody Allen's advice that 80 percent of life is showing up. Students don't regard such a situation nearly as seriously as a teacher. They haven't failed anything, and they're having a good time. Unless a teacher is mean to them or tries too much to exert control he obviously doesn't have, they won't make trouble for him outside of the room. The same, by the way, cannot always be said for colleagues who might witness his difficulties.

However, various reasons can cause students to want to strike out against a teacher. For one thing, nobody likes to be humbled, especially before others. A leader who is humiliated will almost always retaliate unless most of his group think the shaming is deserved. One boy, a fearless and quite popular leader, nevertheless always teased his fellow classmates mercilessly about the errors on their papers. When they read each other's paragraphs, he pointed out invariably if good-naturedly that so-and-so was illogical, somebody else incoherent, still somebody else ungrammatical. It happened that he himself was a horrible speller and when he once submitted a paper with "intelligents" written for "intelligence," his teacher could not resist sharing his blunder with his classmates, who laughed uproariously. He laughed, too, if rather sheepishly.

In another class, though, the leader tried to impress his classmates and his teacher at the beginning of the year with what he thought were sophisticated answers. His teacher felt that he was simply hogging the discussion and that his answers were simplistic. Her tone of voice and her glances conveyed that she did not particularly esteem this student. He read her cues. Often loud and obnoxious, he and his troops were especially delighted to discover any point that the teacher couldn't explain or to confuse her explanations. Because the teacher didn't understand their subtle harassment, she thought she hadn't prepared well enough.

Leader or not, any student will be likely to demean his teacher if that is the only way the student can exit from a tight spot gracefully. It makes no difference either if he has boxed himself in or if his teacher has cornered him. One student was trying to impress his friends with accounts of his latest feats. The teacher told him to get busy. Several minutes later the teacher issued a second warning, since there had been no improvement. The boy muttered to his pal something like, "She'll have to make me if she wants me to shut up." As he intended, the teacher and most of the rest of the class heard his taunt. A showdown was then almost inevitable, since the student wanted to fight. When he was finally sent from the room, the results were predictable. Slamming the door, the boy screamed an obscenity at his teacher.

What makes a student pick a fight isn't always clear. Maybe something or someone was bothering the boy, and he took it out on the teacher. Maybe he just didn't want to work that day. In any event, because he was guilty of rank insubordination before the rest of the class, he was forced to apologize to his teacher before he rejoined the group. In such cases students often think that the teacher is upset merely because of the vulgarity, but that's not it at all. Before their careers are over, most teachers hear themselves referred to in many unflattering ways. If the curses are uttered privately and in anger, they're not usually singled out for special offense. It's the public challenge to authority that cannot be brooked. Other students wait to hear what the teacher has done about it, and they will find out by the time the offender returns to class.

Students with special ability occasionally think they can force a teacher to tolerate almost any kind of behavior. This is especially true of stars in acting, music, or sports. One coach was having difficulty in getting his team members to show up on time for games. The next game was to be at another school. He announced that the bus would leave a certain place at four o'clock and that only those on the bus by that time would play. The first-string quarterback, however, must have thought that this stipulation did not apply to him, since the local newspaper had proclaimed that he was the primary reason for the team's winning streak. On the day of the game, the quarterback arrived at school five minutes after four, just as the bus was pulling out of the parking lot. Sprinting after it, he jumped aboard as the driver slowed down for him. The coach, however, ordered him off the bus. Instead he smiled incredulously and sat down. When the coach approached the boy's seat and once more told him to get off the bus, he stood up and punched the coach in the mouth. Fortunately, several other players pulled the boy back to his seat and then they, the driver, and the coach literally carried the quarterback off the bus. And he was off the team too for the rest of that season.

Unlike these last two cases, justice is sometimes on the students' side when they insult or strike a teacher. If a teacher is inconsistent in his behavior toward students, if he falsely accuses them, or if he is otherwise unkind to them, they would all like to retaliate. They will do so, depending on how angry they become, how much they fear a teacher, and what recourse they think they have.

One teacher started her first job determined to be as close to as many students as she could. She talked with them in the halls between classes, she ate her lunch at their tables, and she encouraged them to visit her in her office. In these ways she thought she would be able to help them with their personal problems. Her classes were always noisy, but she thought that this indicated a healthy atmosphere. One day, though, there was a great deal of work to be done, and the leader of the group wouldn't settle down. Because he kept interrupting with silly wisecracks, the teacher couldn't get on with the lesson. In exasperation she told him to sit down and be quiet. When he advised her with an oath not to tell *him* to "shut up," she retorted that he was not to speak to her that way. That remark made him shout: "I don't understand you. One minute you're acting as if you're one of us and the next you're pulling this teacher routine. It doesn't work that way, you know."

This boy's reaction reminds me of my relationship with one of my former principals. He vacillated between being almost overly friendly and being haughtily aloof. As a result I never knew where I stood with him. Similarly it's unfair to students for a teacher to pretend he's one of them or that all votes are equal in the classroom unless the teacher will abide by those conditions all of the time. A teacher who expects ever to be able to insist on a certain kind of behavior from students soon learns that maintaining a friendly reserve makes that easier. This is one reason why most teachers won't allow students to call them by their first names, even when the teacher's own age happens to be very close to that of the students.

Another sure way to ask for trouble is, unwittingly or not, to accuse a student unjustly. I would like to think that such accusations result from teachers seeing incidents incorrectly. I know too, though, that some teachers feel they can't admit their errors even when they are aware of them. Since the following case was relayed to me by the student involved, I can't account for the motivation of his teacher. As the boy later surmised, the trouble may have started because his teacher sized him up as an obedient student. He remembered a day when the teacher had noticed a crumpled wad of paper beside the student's desk. "Who threw that paper on the floor?" the teacher asked. Nobody said anything. He then looked at the boy and demanded, "Did you throw it down?"

"No, sir."

"Well, you pick it up anyway," he barked. The boy complied without thinking because he had been taught to be respectful of his teachers.

Another day before the teacher came into the class, some students were tossing a Frisbee around the room. Suddenly a windowpane shattered. Even though the boy in question had not been playing, someone quickly tossed him the Frisbee. And before he could throw it to someone else, the teacher appeared. Without queries, he commanded the boy to give him the Frisbee and report to the principal. The boy handed over the toy but told the teacher he had not been playing; the Frisbee had been thrown to him only at the moment the teacher arrived. Since no one in the room volunteered to confirm his story, however, the boy complied with the teacher's instructions.

The unpleasantness between the two came to a climax one day just before the start of an assembly. Students were filing into the auditorium. The boy, as well as some others from the class, had found places and were talking. All at once, one of them hit the fellow next to him on the side of the head, that boy returned the blow, and then punches flew wildly. It looked as if this might well be the start of a serious fight, but by the time their teacher arrived, all was quiet. A student had signaled his approach. The teacher accused the same boy he had held responsible for the Frisbee incident of throwing the first punch. Twice the student contradicted the charge. In fact, the boy became quite determined not to give in this time, since he was convinced his teacher picked on him. The several minutes of loud and angry words next exchanged between them had begun to attract much more attention than the original fracas before the teacher finally declared, "You follow me, young man."

Instead of following him, the falsely accused boy slapped the teacher across the mouth. Other teachers quickly rushed to the aid of their colleague, and the boy was subdued by some fellow students, even though others jubilantly cheered him. He was then escorted to the principal's office, where he was interrogated for a long time. Through it all the boy stood his ground: he maintained his innocence and also refused to name the students who were guilty. Apparently somewhat amazed at the vehemence of this normally mild-mannered youth, the principal told him that regardless of his guilt or innocence, he would have to apologize to the teacher for hitting him. Since the student's ire had been sufficiently provoked, though, he refused this as well. He said he would be suspended, as the principal threatened, rather than submit.

It's difficult not to conclude that this teacher was particularly arrogant. We heard only the boy's version of the story, though, and it would also be interesting to know how confident the teacher was of his accusation. A teacher soon becomes accustomed to students denying what he sees or hears them do or say. When a teacher first encounters such protestations of innocence, he may doubt his own senses, but it doesn't take long to realize that many students blatantly lie. However, in addition to the possible moral error, this teacher committed a definite pedagogical one. He should never have allowed a confrontation like that to blossom before the entire student body. After the boy emphatically denied the charge, there was little chance he would back down in front of his friends. That's the moment to order him out of the assembly. The teacher and student can then privately discuss the trouble, and whatever happens will almost always be preferable to a public display like this one. There are really only two reasons why teachers should ever resort to outside help in discipline problems. One, they may feel they lack the physical strength or authority to settle an incident by themselves, or, two, they wish to make an example of the offender because of the seriousness of the misbehavior. Students always view a case where the principal is called in more seriously than other ones; on the other hand, students don't respect a teacher who's always having to rely on outside help.

The example also shows that a teacher's attitude toward his students more than anything else determines whether they will look on him as unkind or harsh. Sometimes teachers who might appear to outsiders as quite rough or gruff aren't perceived that way at all by their students. A teacher at one school objected to male students wearing hats inside the building. Whenever he saw a boy with one on, he would order him to take it off. If the boy didn't obey at once, the teacher himself would usually snatch the hat from his head. This teacher was regarded by the students as strict and old-fashioned, but he was not seen as unkind. Even the boy who took issue with him about it and forced a confrontation in the principal's office simply thought him an outmoded busybody.

One day another teacher lost patience with a boy who had been disruptive just a little too long; suddenly she began pelting that boy with blows. Contrary to what usually happens when a student is disciplined in any form, though, the rest of the class seemed uninterested. They apparently thought the boy deserved the teacher's chastisement. And they wanted both the teacher and the boy to be quiet so they could hear the film they were watching. Since another teacher was also in the room, he took charge of the group, sending the first teacher scurrying to the principal.

The principal, guidance counselor, and teacher agreed that the best way to settle the incident and hopefully avoid a lawsuit was to remove the student from the teacher's class. Accordingly the transfer was effected at once, but the next day the boy appeared at the teacher's departmental office asking for her. As she went to meet him, she thought, "Well, I'm in for it this time." To her great surprise, however, the student wasn't seeking any kind of reprisal; rather he wanted to be reinstated in her class. Admitting that he had been wrong, he even volunteered that she could also hit him the next time he was out of line if she wouldn't be "unfair" and kick him out of class. He said he didn't think he'd been "bad" enough to deserve that. It's not, then, so much what a teacher does that will cause students to think him a tyrant, but whether his actions and attitudes seriously threaten their human dignity.

Importantly, a teacher's attitude must not convey favoritism. Personal likes and dislikes should not enter into matters of discipline, although it's generally agreed that maintaining order is easier if a friendly atmosphere prevails. Should a teacher find himself disliking most of his students, that's probably cause for him to examine his vocation. I remember reading comments by one teacher who had worked in a neighborhood school for some thirty years. She had seen the ethnic composition of the community change several times since she had started work there, and she was very dissatisfied with its present make-up. Her prejudice, condescension, and ill will were implicit in almost every remark she made about the students she was then teaching. To her, those first-graders were little better than animals, an attitude surely projected to them.

Even when a teacher may not especially despise his students, belittlement of them is a habit that's easy to fall into. His work forces him to deal with students' inadequacies. No one, however, likes to hear that he's an arrant simpleton for what he doesn't know or can't do. A teacher need only consider how it would feel to be on the receiving end of disparaging remarks to realize why they anger students so. One boy's handwriting was particularly difficult to decipher; he realized this and usually typed his reports. When he was unable to do this on one occasion, his teacher screamed at him unmercifully. "How dare you waste my time with this scribble?" she complained. "A moron could write better. Were you blindfolded when you were taught to write? Anyone can see that this paper is impossible to read so don't expect me to grade it." A hush fell over the room following this outburst, and the boy's face turned beet red. Although the teacher had every right to refuse to grade a report she couldn't read, the fury impelling her sarcastic tirade had little if anything to do with the illegibility of the report. Several other students even told the teacher, who was generally well liked by her students, that she was being cruel.

Except in extreme cases students usually will not retaliate for wrongs unless a teacher has proven himself weak. Occasionally a teacher's hesitancy is so marked that he appears almost to fear students. Even innocent questions fluster him, not to speak of teasing. Perhaps he is wishy-washy about acceptable classroom behavior, as well as punishment of misbehavior. Perhaps he threatens more discipline than he is capable of delivering. Sometimes a teacher is powerless in gaining a group's confidence and cooperation because he is unaware of who the troublemakers in the group are. To be respected a teacher must convey that he understands what is taking place in the room and how to get students to do what they should.

A teacher who is simply weak can expect plenty of mischief from students, but one who is weak and also unkind can expect retribution. Students know that they have a good chance of getting away with whatever they do to a defenseless teacher, and they feel they have justice on their side. Their retaliations, most often mischief intended to hurt a teacher personally, usually cannot be blamed on any one person. In one case a neat teacher who had constantly berated her students for their slovenliness came to class three days in a row to find the contents of the trash basket strewn on top of her desk. She never discovered who was responsible for the disarray, and the only way she could seem to stop it was to arrive in the room before the teacher who preceded her had left. Another teacher who had promised students they would be graded by one standard but in actuality graded them by another found her office in a shambles one day. Nothing was stolen, but the files were emptied of their contents and all the furniture was askew. Treatment like this should warn a teacher that something in his own character may be amiss. If he can't change his attitudes toward students, there will be a nagging recurrence of "tricks" like these. Perhaps the person would be better suited to another career, a decision more easily made before too much time and effort are invested in teaching.

Problems of Student Interaction

Calling excessive talking and laughter a problem may seem naïve in an age when classroom crimes occur, yet anybody who has ever been to school has probably been reprimanded for just such friendly interchanges. The difficulty arises because students don't seem to know when to stop conversing and they think it's a teacher's job to make them stop. Much leniency indicates to them that a teacher doesn't know how to do that or else doesn't care.

When corrected for talking, many students have a standard alibi. Whether the teacher is lecturing or the class discussing an issue, they were "asking about the lesson." Apparently this plea has been successful enough in the past for students almost inevitably to think it may work again. Until they realize that a teacher sees through such ruses and until they become convinced that he means what he says, no amount of asking or telling them to be quiet will do any good.

Some teachers advocate reasoning to persuade students to leave off their socializing, but I wonder if that counseling isn't largely a waste of time. High school students surely realize that they're supposed to work in classes. The simplest solution is probably to separate neighbors who can't stop talking. Even though this correction may sound more appropriate for elementary school than for high school, many adults use a variation of the same technique when they rid their house of all sweets before they start a diet. In any event, changing the seating arrangement is a correction students usually don't resist very much. When it works, as it often does, a teacher has solved the problem without overtime for himself or his students.

Naturally, if too many couples need separation, a teacher must seek another solution. Most students will be motivated to work more and socialize less if they are graded frequently on material covered in class. These quizzes, which are helpful for reasons other than disciplining students, don't have to be long, but they allow students to grasp a connection between their marks and their behavior. While a teacher doesn't grade poor conduct, most students will soon see that it may lead to poor grades.

Solutions like these won't ever eliminate personal chatter in a classroom, but they will discourage it. The procedures are good, too, because a teacher applies them without asking anyone for help. Of course, if he could dismiss a student from the room until he agrees to behave, that would be best. In public schools, though, a teacher can't simply send anyone from the room; he must send him to a disciplinary officer. When a teacher opts to send very many students out of the room for misbehavior as negligible as talking too much, it is a good indication to students and administrators that the teacher is unsure of what he's doing.

The socializing in a roomful of friends can be a nuisance, but the trouble is minor when compared to the turmoil that can exist when students don't get along with each other. It often appears at first that there's much more unfriendliness in a school than there really is. Most boys especially like to scuffle with their friends. Thus, even though one student's grabbing or shoving or even tripping or hitting another might cause an uproar in a class, that does not necessarily signal hostility any more than would one adult's slapping another on the back.

Serious physical fights are still rare in most classrooms. People generally don't often resort to physical violence to settle their disputes, perhaps less because of scruples than because of fear of consequences. If a fight does erupt in a classroom, everything else stops until order is restored. A teacher, though, is no more responsible for physically ending a fight than he would be for putting out a fire should that occur. One incident in which two students became enraged enough with each other to slug it out occurred during homeroom. The teacher had finished the roll call and announcements and was glancing over her notes for the next period's class. Sensing trouble, she looked up to see two students, fists drawn, squaring up to each other in the back of the room. She got up from her desk at once and walked toward the boys, ordering them to stop. By this time, though, the boys were exchanging earnest blows and seemed totally oblivious to the teacher's second command to stop. Two other boys then pulled the fighters apart, obviating the teacher's decision to call the office for help.

After everything had calmed down, one of the fighters tried to convince the teacher that their fight hadn't been serious enough for them to be sent to the principal. Probably trying to see if contrition might soften his teacher's heart, he said he was sorry he had started the fight and wouldn't do so again. He added that they had just been quarreling about a broken pencil. Even though the teacher had no way of knowing exactly how much of this explanation was true, it was clear to her that the school's regular procedure should be followed in this case. All students expected the principal to handle instances of fighting; all had witnessed the repeated blows. All knew the boys had not been joking, since no students would be likely to break up an encounter that was simply friendly sparring. Had this teacher failed to send those two boys to the principal, not only would she have assumed responsibility that was not hers, but she also would have jeopardized future orderliness in the class.

Many students, including those who consider themselves too sophisticated to fight physically, are quite willing to hurt others psychologically. Emotional "stabbing," a more subtle kind of student conflict, must usually be resolved by the classroom teacher if it is to end. Sometimes these cases evolve around one or two individuals singled out for abuse by the rest. In other situations groups of students battle for power. Why people should want to hurt others is intriguing. Apparently a certain kind of excitement can be derived from watching others' discomfort; we are aroused by it while feeling safe ourselves. Moreover, leaders recognize that their authority may be enhanced by sanctioning infliction of suffering, even though it is a risky tactic. A leader gains added allegiance in this way if enough of his followers are convinced to go along with him. They are bound to a leader who makes them feel justified in the cruelty they would like to practice anyway but somehow feel they shouldn't.

The leader selects the victims. When one or two individuals in a group are singled out by its leader for punishment, they usually differ from most of the others in the group. The leader personally may contemn or envy that difference, but he believes he can persuade most of his group to scorn it. They know that they can be relatively secure in venting disapproval, since even a person of strong character finds it difficult to withstand the taunts of a group. And if a person is embarrassed about the characteristic or condition that sets him apart, his embarrassment often renders him defenseless.

Most high school leaders may not consciously understand this reasoning, but they still manipulate situations to their advantage. For one thing, they know how to choose the right moment to act. A class leader realizes that at times a teacher will be reluctant to correct offenders on the spot, since to do so would further humiliate the student already being ridiculed. Such an occasion arose in one class when students were reporting about their research on various sociological topics. The victim, an intense fifteen-year-old rather mortified about her overweight, was absorbed in her report on future space colonies. Suddenly the teacher heard the leader snickering about the speaker's quite large derrière in tones loud enough for everyone to hear. As various students began to giggle, the fat girl, visibly flustered, finished her report as quickly as she could and sat down. The leader surely understood that the teacher would spare the victim's feelings by overlooking this insult in class. If the teacher reprimanded the leader later, what would this or even more severe punishment mean in comparison to the "fun" she and her companions had already had in class?

In fact, the teacher acted exactly as the leader had anticipated.

The leader held a trump too. When the teacher confronted her after school with her shamelessness, she denied responsibility because once again she knew that she could get away with it. She was certain that since she had sat a number of rows behind the teacher, the teacher couldn't positively blame her. Not until a week or two later did the teacher begin to give this leader her comeuppance. It happened that the teacher wore unstylish corrective oxfords most of the time because her feet were somewhat malformed. The leader mistakenly assumed that the teacher would be as reticent about her shoes as the fat girl had been about her posterior. *Sotto voce* the leader commented, "What lovely shoes . . . and a different pair to match every dress." Grins hardly had time to appear on her friends' faces before the teacher, with all the fury of a cripple wronged, marched to the student's desk, stood over her, and retorted, "Lovely enough to kick you with." She had no intention of touching the girl, but the girl didn't know that.

Shocked and subdued by her teacher's indignation, the leader whimpered that she was sorry. She added that she had only been joking. The teacher was unreceptive to the feeble apology, however, and replied, "You may be kidding, but I'm not. You and your friends are not going to mock me or anyone else in this room anymore." All the while she hovered over the student, by her very presence threatening physical retaliation. The leader's fear of this, combined with her loss of face before peers, was sufficient to suppress her crude behavior.

In another instance a senior boy was openly scorned in class by his fellow students. Whenever he tried to speak in a discussion, various of his classmates would enter private conversations. Some even laughed outright at him no matter what he said. The boy himself somewhat aggravated the conflict because the more others mocked or seemingly ignored him, the more determined he became not to be intimidated. When a victim is singled out like this, the teacher's task is to discover why. The individual is being taunted because he's different from the others, and if that difference is not apparent physically, it usually will be in his likes and dislikes or in his way of life. In this case, as it turned out, a large part of the problem was that this boy was still a Boy Scout, still a paper boy, still a builder of model airplanes after most of the rest of them had long since given up these activities.

Until the teacher decided to confront the students openly about their cruelty, his remonstrances for order were only partially successful. He knew that to broach the subject directly would be added chagrin for the boy, but the teacher's concern was to save the class. At first, various students quickly denied any knowledge of what the teacher was talking about. In time, though, some reluctantly admitted that they were teasing the boy. The leader of the group then maintained that the boy "deserved" the treatment he got. Although the teacher realized that their behavior was most likely directed at forcing the boy to give up what they thought were childish hobbies, nevertheless, the classroom is not the place for blatant and repeated ridicule. However, instead of discussing these complex matters with the group, the teacher asked, "Does this person deserve to be mocked because he likes to do things you don't? Would any one of you like to be scorned for something you like to do?"

A teacher who thus challenges a group runs a risk. If he can't convince them to change, he will appear foolish and conditions will worsen. There are essentially two ways, though, to ameliorate such situations. One is to convince the group not to go along with the leader, and the other is to convince the leader personally to stop. The plan one chooses depends largely on the nature of the problem. When a group ridicules a person for a physical abnormality, most members can feel at a safe distance. They don't really empathize with being fat or crippled or something like that. Therefore it would be unwise to try to convince a group not to go along with the leader. However, when a person is singled out for abuse because of his likes and dislikes, everyone in the group must be on guard. No one is truly free to do something that will be unapproved by the group. All can see how easy it would be for the "sport" to turn on them.

Much more difficult for a teacher to deal with are those problems resulting from groups of students seeking to dominate each other. The smaller social units of every student body, sometimes called cliques, sometimes clubs, sometimes gangs, form along the ethnic, racial, religious, economic, and other social indicators of its community, as well as on other interests such as athletics and drama. A community divided ethnically or racially will have those same rifts in its school. These divisions do not always affect a classroom teacher, though, even when large numbers of conflicting groups are in a class. He becomes concerned only if one group tries to exert its control over another so as to take charge of the class.

The immediate question in a teacher's mind probably is how he can recognize this kind of situation. As one would expect, members of a group usually stay together physically. They often enter the class at the same time, sit beside each other if possible, leave together, and look to one of their members as a spokesman. To express dominance, a group may use any type of ridicule that is convenient, be it religious, ethnic, or any other topic. The major issue is the attempt of one group to subdue the other, not the lines along which the dominance is formed. Slurs are not always said for a teacher to hear, but when they occur he along with all the students detects tension in the atmosphere. Importantly, too, when these problems arise, they seldom disappear by themselves. The teacher must demonstrate that he, not a clique or gang, is in charge of what happens in the room.

In one instance a leader of a group tried to splinter a class in relation to the religious backgrounds of its members. There were some twenty Christians in this class, largely Catholic, with five or six Jews. Sometime in the beginning of the year the leader of the Christians, an Irish Catholic, singled out one of the Jews as an easy mark. One day before class the Irish Catholic said lightheartedly but loudly, "What's a nice Jewish boy like you doing with long red hair?" The response to his mockery was a blush— the boy was also the only redhead in the class. The teacher was surprised at the slur but ignored it since class wasn't in session.

When another jibe was forthcoming a few days later, the teacher understood that the likelihood of trouble existed. On this day the teacher was tongue-lashing the class for being unprepared. When she had finished, the leader popped out laughingly, "How can a

Jewish mother allow her son to come to school unprepared?" Once more the Jew blushed and was silent. Without thinking, though, the teacher snapped back, "The same reason Irish Catholic mothers do." She hoped that her sarcastic response-in-kind would teach the leader what it felt like to be mocked.

Her idea was unsuccessful. The leader didn't seem at all embarrassed. He laughed, probably finding it amusing that the teacher was also emphasizing the religious polarity in the class. Several days later, when the Irish Catholic was ready with yet another of his "jovial" taunts for the Jew, moral as well as professional instinct told the teacher to find a way to stop the jeers. In cases like this, a teacher usually begins by privately admonishing the leader that the teacher understands exactly what he's up to and why; sometimes a person can be genuinely shamed for insensitivity merely by being forced to acknowledge the intent of his words. If he isn't, a teacher may then combine shaming with scaring. Has a student like this considered that his slurs can boomerang on him? Has he wondered why his classmates did not join him in his taunts? Is it possible that others may start regarding him as an emotional cripple who compensates for his own inadequacies by trying to lower others?

In another class rival groups formed, quite incidentally, along economic lines. They were both middle class, but contrary to what one might expect, the less affluent of the two dominated by making the other feel inferior. While the teacher recognized the existence of the cliques early in the year, he didn't realize there was a problem until January and then didn't know how to deal with it successfully. As he related the story to me, his first clue should have been when he himself started to dread to go to this class. A teacher does not dread a class merely because some students are noisy, as these were; that's a rather normal hazard of his trade to which he soon builds up immunity. He didn't want to go to that class because he, like one of the groups of students, felt humiliated by the other group. One day the class had studied an eighteenth-century work in which the term "Brownists" appeared. Since the name was unimportant to what was being taught, the teacher had not researched it and did not identify it. The leader pertly said, "Of course you're going to explain who the Brown-ists were." When the teacher responded with all he knew about this faction, namely, that it was a group of seventeenth-century Englishmen who criticized the established church, the leader pur-sued her course with, "That's so superficial. Can't you tell us what they really did?" Even though he was well prepared for that particular lesson and for all others too, the teacher felt guilty and blushed. The leader, though, smiled smugly and leaned back in her chair.

Had the teacher reacted rationally rather than emotionally, he might have begun to question that leader's intentions then and there. Reason should certainly have told him that he had no cause to be ashamed and that the student was impolite. What he might have done was decline to answer her question in class and to invite her to discuss it privately later. No one can logically object to such a postponement since it is obvious that basic issues, more than obscure details, must be covered in class. More-over, a private conference allows a teacher to concentrate on the manner in which a question is asked as well as what is asked and hence to evaluate the sincerity of the query. Generally, only stu-dents who truly want to learn will be interested enough to ap-pear for conferences. A student whose questions are motivated by a desire to ridicule a teacher or other students will almost never come for private discussions because he understands that his de-rision will lose most of its sting if he has no audience. Many students, too, who appear quite bold before the class become much less audacious when they meet the teacher alone. They realize they're subject to individual scrutiny by someone who has some authority over them.

However, since the teacher in this case allowed the leader to embarrass him one time without doing anything about it, sel-dom a day passed after that when she or one of her group didn't try to discover an inadequacy in his preparation. Apparently he never consciously understood what they were up to even though he was plagued enough by the situation to dream about it. He did nothing else, though. While he correctly felt responsible that the class wasn't going well, he never understood why. Importantly, the teacher failed to see the similarity between what this leader was doing to him and what she was doing to other members of the class. She and her clique were mocking the attitudes and work of the rival faction just as they were ridiculing the teacher. The subdued group had ceased contributing to class discussions and started talking among themselves after they had been subjected to a barrage of condescending remarks, the impact of which the teacher didn't realize. Members of the dominant group would slight their classmates superciliously with remarks such as: "That's not right. How can you possibly think *that*?" or "Haven't you heard of *that* book?" Like their teacher, the students felt intimidated by this intellectual snobbery, and like him, they didn't know what to do about it.

To remedy a situation deteriorated to that extent, a teacher would have to convince all of the students that an answer to any question can be shown to be superficial or in some way unsatisfactory if that is one's intent. Had the teacher merely probed the answers of the members of this clique, they could have been made to appear as foolish and unsophisticated as they were making the rest of the class feel. While a method like this may at first seem as unprofessional as it is unkind, one need only ask if it is professional or if it is kind to most students to let the circumstances go unaltered. Moreover, it usually doesn't require much turning of the tables to end the condescension. The dominating group becomes less inclined to use a ploy that hurts as much as it helps, the remainder of the class sees that there is no reason to feel inferior, and the energies expended by all on the psychological warfare can then be redirected toward more suitable ends.

Immoral and Illegal Behavior

In some classrooms today both students and teachers live almost constantly with the threat of physical assault. While happily this extreme condition doesn't generally prevail, all modern teachers deal with numerous instances of student immorality and, less frequently, criminality. Probably the most common of these is cheating.

When I began teaching, my attitude was that most students were honest. My years in the classroom, however, have not borne out that benign appraisal. One convincing experience occurred in the fall of my first year of teaching. After students were settled into a test, I decided to step out into the hall for a drink of water. A colleague happened by and we chatted for two or three minutes. When I re-entered the classroom, most of my students were discussing the answers. I did not punish those students, since I was guilty of a procedural error; I simply composed another test for them. Never again, though, have I left a class unattended during testing, even for a few moments.

There is nothing new about various forms of cheating inside or outside schools. What may be different about cheating in this century is our attitude toward it. Like many of the adults around them, students often see no immorality at all in the action. Many of them are not even shamed by being apprehended. They worry only when they realize that being caught may affect their grades. During an examination in one class, the teacher saw a student take a notebook from inside her desk and openly copy from that onto her test paper. He caught the girl's eye, looked at her sadly, and smiled. Several days after the exam when he returned her paper with a zero on it, she seemed astounded and asked him about it after class. This man, educated in the old-fashioned way, thought that the facts that he had seen the student cheat and that she knew he had seen her were sufficient for the student to understand that she would receive no credit for the test. She, however, expected him to take her notebook from her or at least order her to put it away. She interpreted his silence and his failure to do anything immediately to mean that it was all right for her to cheat.

Several years ago I was somewhat astonished to hear students of mine discuss a story about a boy expelled from school for cheating. Almost to a person, they identified with that likable chap, as the author of the story intended. But most failed to grasp the author's point that the lack of preparation prompting the cheating resulted from the boy's own laziness. He had earlier signed an honor code not to cheat and he had sworn on the examination in question that he had not cheated on it, knowing that cheating automatically carried the penalty of expulsion. Nevertheless, my students felt the school was much too harsh for refusing him another chance. As we were finishing our discussion, one student admitted that naturally she'd cheat to improve her grade. "What did you expect?" she asked.

Regardless of a teacher's personal views about cheating, he has no choice but to try to prevent it in classes. Not only is evaluating learning impossible when cheating goes unchecked, but letting it flourish is also the quickest way to destroy student morale. The burden of proof, though, lies with the teacher. Perhaps some time ago teachers might have been free to rip up papers whenever they suspected students of wrongdoing, but these are the times of lawsuits against teachers. Most find that it's easier to prevent cheating on exams than to prove it. One way to discourage cheating is to move physically around the room while proctoring. Another way is to give nonobjective forms of tests or several variations of the same objective test.

However, a teacher cannot always witness the actual occurrence of cheating even though he has evidence that it took place. Assume that a teacher reads an answer to a question and he notices its similarity to another answer he has already read. On comparing the two papers, he discovers that they are almost alike. When this happens, I usually call together after school all the students involved and require them to write a second and more difficult examination under my supervision. The second examination is the one that counts and the students are not penalized for the first. Although this approach certainly demands additional work on my part, it soon helps to curb the problem because word gets around that it's hard to get away with cheating.

One form of cheating, plagiarism, often necessitates a great deal of additional work by the teacher in locating the sources that were used. Some students are uninformed about what plagiarism means; they think that if they change a word or two in a passage they have somehow made that passage their own. Others who know perfectly well that they are stealing think that their copying has a good chance of being undetected; many imagine that unless a teacher happens to be familiar with the book from which they have copied, he won't know they have plagiarized. They obviously don't realize that it is necessary to read only a few sets of student papers to be able to distinguish the usual style in those from that of professional writers.

The easiest way to treat most instances of plagiarism is to talk with the student privately about the seriousness of plagiarism, ask him to bring to another conference the source or sources he used, and explain that he will be given a second chance to prepare his paper. If the student acknowledges what he has done, as many will at this point, the teacher is spared the task of tracking down the source. Reluctant students will sometimes admit plagiarism by being asked to define difficult words in the passage. When a student has to acknowledge that he doesn't know what something means, he can hardly maintain that he wrote it.

Some students, though, will not admit that they have plagiarized until a teacher produces the source from which they copied. They may also try to attack the teacher for impugning their character by the accusation. I recall a particularly involved case like this some years back. A student presented a paper to me that I was certain was copied but for which I didn't know the sources. When I asked her about it, she insisted that she was aware of the meaning of plagiarism, that she had read books as she thought about her topic, but that the ideas and writing in the paper were her own. As I requested, she brought to me several days later the five or six books she said she had used, and together we examined relevant passages in them, comparing those to her paper. Nothing matched. Nevertheless, even though she would not budge from her position that the paper was her own work, I was positive it was not. I told her I would have to delay giving her a grade until I could check other sources in the library.

While this remained unresolved, she presented to me another and longer paper. To my amazement, I immediately saw that once again parts were plagiarized. This time when I confronted her, she indignantly turned on me, trying to make me uncertain about my charge. She claimed that she had worked hard in my class and that as the end of our time together neared I had no right to suggest that she was a poor student or one who would act so reprehensibly. She also pointed out that I knew her work well and had myself often praised it as outstanding. What she did not realize was that my very familiarity with her work was what convinced me she was incapable of the papers she had submitted.

About a month later, after she had threatened that her parents were thinking of consulting their lawyer, I found the book from which she had copied. When I showed the student the passages, she of course had to abandon her earlier pose of righteous indignation. This time she cried. She would never have done such a thing, she said, had she not been under so much pressure. She sniveled that she hoped I would not look on her as a cheat, because she really wasn't. It seemed fairly obvious, though, that her contrition was intended to manipulate me as much as she had hoped her earlier accusations would. She was not truly repentant for what she had done; rather she was sorry that her last term's grade would be a C instead of her usual A.

Whenever a student's grade is to be affected that much by cheating, it is customary for an administrator to be consulted about and to approve of the teacher's decision in the case. Naturally, no administration advocates cheating, but for various reasons they may be unwilling to support a teacher's harsh punishment of it. This does not mean that a teacher has to compromise his own standards, but it may mean that he has to allow a student another chance to master the material or to rewrite the paper.

A second and entirely different form of student wrongdoing is that stemming from use of alcohol or drugs. Whatever the morality of the matter, use of alcohol and drugs is illegal for minors in most states. Nevertheless, use of these substances is widespread among teen-agers and is sometimes evident in the classroom. Unless students are inexperienced with whatever it is they are consuming, though, they usually don't present a behavioral problem in class. They're not eager to have their misdemeanor come to anyone's attention.

One story involving a novice took place on a hot day in late spring. Apparently several sixteen-year-olds accustomed to their beers invited an inexperienced boy to join them for a round. When the three returned to school and their afternoon class, the boy who was new to it all found everything that anybody said terribly funny. For a time he just could not stop laughing. Gradually, however, he became more and more subdued and then, hand over mouth, he burst from the room. Ten minutes or so later when he returned, he was quite pale and unsteady. The teacher realized that the boy, as well as the two others, had almost certainly been drinking.

Although school policies differ slightly, it is almost never a classroom teacher's responsibility to discipline students for alcohol or drugs unless they are also disorderly. Instead he reports suspected users to appropriate school authorities, who, in turn, decide what should be done. In the above example the teacher warned the boy who had caused the slight commotion that he had better mend his ways. The teacher said nothing to the other two boys, but he had previously reported them to the vice-principal because their behavior on a number of occasions had suggested intoxication. Sometimes teachers, who must be concerned about all of their students, wonder why any student obviously and repeatedly using alcohol or drugs should be allowed to remain in a class or in school. A teacher, though, doesn't make that decision, and he doesn't always know all the facts. Perhaps the students are receiving treatment; perhaps there is no other institution to absorb them.

Of all school crimes, theft is the one most likely to occur in a class. An example happened just before the start of a week's vacation. Because one teacher was leaving town that afternoon, she had more cash with her than she normally carried. Nevertheless, as was her custom when she taught, she stored her pocketbook in her classroom in one of her unlocked desk drawers. At various times that morning she moved away from her desk to supervise students at their desks. During those moments her pocketbook was unattended and exposed, for her policy was to permit any student to go to her desk for supplies whether or not she was there. At noon that day she discovered that her wallet with over three hundred dollars in it had been taken from her purse. School officials summoned police, who began that afternoon to interrogate her students. But she had taught some seventy-five people that morning, and there was no definite evidence that the theft had occurred while her classes were in session. Given such scant clues, police were unable to solve this crime. Some people insist students will act according to the expectations their teachers hold for them. If this is true, though, why was that teacher robbed? She obviously thought she could trust all of her students.

The most serious behavioral problems in a school, including vandalism, narcotics peddling, and even murder, usually do not occur in classrooms, at least not when classes are in session, and hence seldom directly involve classroom teachers as such. The perpetrators may not even be enrolled in the school. If a teacher witnesses or is subject to a crime in school, he acts just as he would were he any place else. He does all he reasonably can to protect other innocent persons as well as himself, and he alerts the administration or police at once.

Fostering Desirable Student Behavior

A colleague of mine once laughingly told me that the only worthwhile advice he'd ever been given about teaching came from the man under whom he had practice-taught. The man claimed that a good teacher should be "half blind and half deaf." I laughed too when I first heard this because it often seems that much of the annoyance in teaching results from trying to get students to behave properly. Thinking that over, though, I believe that instead of being half blind, a teacher actually needs "eyes in the back of his head." Even though this cliché is usually associated with unflinchingly strict schoolmarms, an effective teacher must not only see and hear what students are doing, he must also be able to interpret what their actions and words mean. It is one thing for a teacher to decide to ignore a particular instance of misconduct; it is quite another for him to be unaware of it.

That kind of decisiveness results from a teacher's own certainty about what is and what is not acceptable classroom behavior, a certainty acquired before he enters a classroom. Luckily that task becomes less awesome when he concentrates on two rather broad criteria. The classroom is first of all a place for learning, so any behavior interfering with that for very long is inappropriate. Second, any uncivilized behavior is also inappropriate. These two standards, really, are all that are necessary to achieve an orderly classroom. That word "orderly" causes some people's ears to stand up because it used to imply merely silent students. Most educators now realize that while there are times when quiet must be maintained, there are other occasions when an orderly classroom can hum with noise. "Civilized," however, is a more difficult concept to define, even though certain manners like vulgar or rude ones are commonly admitted to be uncivilized. Often to determine whether an action is uncivil, we must look to its underlying motive as well as to its outward appearance. For example, if a student accidentally drops a tissue from his pocket, nobody would define that as uncivilized. The very same end result would be called boorish, though, if a student uses a tissue and throws it on the floor. While the task of civilizing is not exclusively the school's, it is one teachers cannot decline since it is civilized behavior, finally, that makes order possible in a school or any place else where there are numbers of people.

In addition to being clear about how students should act, a teacher must also consider what he will do when students don't conform to acceptable behavior. If he waits until the misbehavior actually occurs before he thinks about his response, he will appear indecisive to students. Suppose, for example, that while a teacher is explaining a problem to the class, he notices a student in the back of the room reading a newspaper. The teacher doesn't say anything at first, but then the student unfolds his paper noisily and spreads it out on his desk. Several other students glance over at him. The teacher now feels it is incumbent upon him to ask the boy to put his paper away. As the boy complies, he mutters, "O.K., Teach. If you say so." The teacher doesn't like the impudent tone of that "teach," but to avoid an issue, he smiles and continues his explanation. The boy soon returns to his reading. This time the teacher says nothing. The next day that boy leaves his paper at home, but two others have theirs. When the teacher tells them to stop reading, one turns to the teacher and says, "Oh yeah. Why're you picking on us? You let so-and-so read yesterday." The teacher doesn't like this student's freshness either, but he admits to himself that what the boy said was true, so he smiles and resumes his lesson. Once more the boys continue reading.

Response like that spells the end of order in a classroom. The teacher has shown that he doesn't know how to get students to do what they should. He is worried about whether he was fair when he should have been concerned about their punk rudeness and defiance. While no administration expects a teacher to keep incorrigible students in class, he is expected to be able to get most of them to behave. Merely avoiding conflict never changes unacceptable student behavior.

Smiling usually doesn't work either. I laugh whenever I hear that advice to teachers about "not smiling before Christmas." But the smile of the teacher in the above example showed he was meekly acquiescing in student misconduct. Unquestionably, he would have found a large physique exuding strength more beneficial than a smile if he wanted to alter their behavior. Not that teachers always have to be physically powerful to be firmly insistent, for as the old saying goes, "It's not so much the size of the dog in the fight as the size of the fight in the dog."

Of course, the classroom behavior that is expected should also be attainable. It's unreasonable to imagine that students will never talk with each other; it's unreasonable to think that they're going to work their heads off every second; it's unreasonable to think that they'll never get into any mischief. A teacher who rigidly tries to impose a standard of conduct that is neither possible nor desirable often provokes as much misconduct as one who is hesitant. Constant barking or whining is just as annoying in a person as it is in an animal. Moreover, overzealousness often indicates a teacher who doesn't distinguish enough among various degrees of misconduct: to him a student's opening his mouth to whisper to a neighbor merits the same kind of correction as wild running about the room. This kind of teacher may be bossy, but he is seldom regarded by students as a true boss.

On the other hand, a teacher whom students will respect is not concerned with getting students to obey him per se so much as he is concerned with getting them to act as they should. A teacher doesn't have to yell at students all the time to accomplish this either, even though raising one's voice from time to time is effective. More important than voice level is a teacher's attitude. It must not matter to him who the student is who is misbehaving; the principal's son is treated the same as the son of anyone else. (Impartiality, incidentally, is easier to talk about than to achieve. Most people find it much more natural to treat the principal's son like any other principal's son.) The teacher must also convey that while he does not enjoy disciplining students, he will if this is the only way they can be convinced to act as they should.

As much as some might like to hope otherwise, no standard of behavior can ever be enforced unless the consequences for failure to conform are as certain—and as spelled out—as they are undesirable. When students don't act properly, they're convinced that nothing much will happen to them for doing as they please. Many Americans are now uncomfortable with the idea that punishment must hurt; they believe this makes the punishment as barbarous as the behavior it seeks to correct. To reason this way, however, is not only to disregard the anarchy that results when a group of people are allowed to act as they wish, but also to fail to understand how people learn. Pain is an essential part of avoidance learning, as validated in animal research. Animals in which the sense of pain is surgically destroyed are unable to learn any avoidance task. This is why a child will not truly be convinced to avoid the flame until he has scorched his finger.

There's no question, therefore, that the threat or the infliction of a sound paddling would improve the conduct of many students. Because we recognize, though, that various motives of people administering whippings can be devious, most states have prohibited this form of correction. And, of course, there are other available and effective measures. No student enjoys being detained before or after school as punishment. Many don't like to have their parents notified about their misbehavior. Most don't like to be suspended or expelled. Obviously a teacher should fit the punishment to the fault, and he should be guided in his selection by the types of punishment the administration supports.

Why, some might ask, must it always be a teacher who sets the standard of behavior? Why shouldn't students participate in deciding what standards should be upheld? Let's analyze this idea by asking another question: why is it that appropriate behavior does not differ very much from class to class, from school to school, or even from country to country? A teacher doesn't invent what is acceptable conduct any more than an orchestra maestro invents the proper speed of any given symphony. Both teacher and conductor have some leeway, of course. But the conductor appears foolish who directs players to perform Beethoven's *Ninth* twice as slowly as its notation indicates. There is, then, no decision to be made about acceptable classroom behavior either by a teacher or by students. Students, though, can help to maintain good classroom conduct. This does not suggest that they should be encouraged to squeal on each other; nothing can be so disgusting as a person willing to tattle because he likes to see others punished or because he is trying to inveigle favors for himself. However, students are always more inclined to listen to each other than they are to a teacher. If one student tells the others to settle down and get back to work, they're apt to do so. Students in a good class often share with the teacher the responsibility for maintaining order.

Pursuing once again the comparison of an orchestra, we see that a good class, like a good orchestra, is one in which all members are working for the same goal. Violinists are required to synchronize the movements of their bows and trumpeters to play more softly not because a conductor is trying to impose his will on them; the orchestra is not *his*. Rather he insists on these things because he wants the orchestra to look and sound as good as it possibly can. It would be unthinkable that one player or section of players be allowed to spoil the work of the entire group. Like a conductor, a teacher wants students to "perform" at their peak. Most students really would like this too, even though they frequently don't know how to go about it. A teacher, therefore, helps them by insisting on orderly classroom behavior that makes the achievement possible.

V
Other Adults in the Building

Students usually do not attend school on the first day; they are also generally excused from the last. It is adults who are there, first to prepare and then to close a session. While this is obvious enough, what lies behind it may not be so apparent. Students pass through a school rather quickly; adults remain. A teacher's relationships with his students will probably determine whether he enjoys his job; his relationships with other adults in the building will determine whether he keeps it.

Almost inevitably periods of new-teacher orientation in schools, as well as college education courses that precede them, assert the benefits a beginner receives from working with an experienced staff. They stress the friendliness and cooperation among staff members. While this is essentially true, these sessions fail to convey other, less evident information that a beginner needs. For instance, how do administrators, veteran teachers, and noninstructional workers really see their work? What do they expect of a new teacher? What is his part on an overall school "team"?

Administration

Ironically, school administrators usually cannot be educators; their duties dictate that they must be business managers. (Names for administrators vary from school to school but include "superintendents," "principals," "deans," and "chairpersons.") As long as schools continue to be controlled locally in this country, administrators will be the chief agents of elected boards of education. No longer the autonomous educators that they might have hoped to be even a half century ago, administrators today generally can't determine what a school will be like. Ultimately, a town decides whether its school is college preparatory or vocationally oriented, whether its policies are conservative, middle-of-the-road, or liberal. To the extent that a chief administrator can fathom what his community wants and produce it for them, he will be liked. To the extent that he tries to sway his community's point of view, his talents as a politician become important.

Thus only secondarily if at all can an administrator concern himself with education. Learning per se has never been highly valued in our pragmatic culture anyway. We measure success more tangibly: we want to know if the learning pays. If it doesn't produce either financial or social gains for a person, we usually consider it rather futile. We worry about a child who prefers his books to his fellows because we think he won't get ahead that way. An administrator's chief worry, then, is not education but the establishment of policies guaranteeing the type of school his board and his community wish. He will be unsuccessful unless he has gathered a staff willing to support those same policies even when they do not wholeheartedly agree with them. And as undesirable as that situation may seem, it means that local citizens largely control their schools, a condition highly preferable to control by centralized bureaucrats and most likely preferable to control by administrators and teachers.

The wisdom of knowing something about a community before one seeks a teaching position in it is evident. If a teacher cannot accept what the community wants and cannot compromise his principles, his job is doomed. This demand for compliance is not modern, either, as Henry David Thoreau quickly found out about 150 years ago in his native Concord, Massachusetts. He defiantly insisted that he would "spare the rod" ironically, by applying it randomly to a half-dozen pupils. Even though Thoreau hoped in this way to demonstrate the unreasonableness of this disciplinary method, his supervisors were unconvinced, and Thoreau resigned a mere few weeks after he had begun. That result was predictable, too, given Thoreau's principles as opposed to the general thinking in Concord about discipline at that time.

If one wishes to keep a job, a saner approach is to find a school whose policies he can support and to express confidence in that school and the persons who administer it. Aside from praise, the option of silence is almost always available too. A beginning teacher, especially, usually finds that after the first week or two of school his opinions are seldom sought.

Some administrative decisions are difficult to appreciate. They may be more readily understood when one remembers that administrators must protect the school as an institution rather than the individuals within it. Several years ago I became enraged about what at first appeared to me a particularly inept administrative decision. Briefly the situation was this. A student I'll call Robert received written notice from his dean that he had cut his English class too many times and that another unexcused absence would be grounds for withdrawal from the course and/or suspension from school. Following that notice, though, Robert cut the class some five or six times, violations the administration ignored. The incident occurred in midwinter and one day a luscious snow covered the ground. A PA announcement, stressed with three repetitions during the day, forbade students to throw snowballs and ominously suggested that doing so would result in suspension. Nevertheless, many youngsters didn't refrain, and one was caught and suspended. Because the injustice of that student's punishment for his first offense, given Robert's repeated offenses, annoyed me, I complained to the dean. That official listened to me politely but offered no explanation for his actions. I suppose that since I was a tenured teacher, my accusation was allowed to be forgotten.

After my anger subsided, some of the rationale for the dean's summary action as opposed to his failure to act occurred to me. Students and teachers may be allowed to hurt themselves individually; even legal codes can't prevent that. The fact that Robert chose to absent himself from class was essentially his problem: it was he who didn't learn and, assuming the importance of the lessons, it will be he who is penalized. No administrative decision to withdraw or suspend him could prevent his personal loss. However, individuals may not be allowed to hurt or to threaten the institution of the school. When the snowball was thrown, the school was threatened because it could be sued if, accidentally or not, that missile injured someone.

There are cases, though, that never appear exactly reasonable. What about the student who went unpunished after falsifying attendance records, an offense punishable by law? Was that leniency prompted because his mother was wealthy and influential? Or what about two instances of pie throwing? The first offender was suspended for twenty-four hours; the second "chose" to withdraw from school. Were those decisions affected by the facts that the first was the son of a noted lawyer and the second a nobody? The list could go on, convincing us that some, usually not many, administrative decisions are inequitable. Without philosophizing about the nature of the world in which we live, we can see that administrators respond to parental and community pressures to keep their jobs. Teachers quickly learn that they do too. Where an administrator draws the line will be determined by many factors, but one of those needn't be the consciences of his staff. An administrator can expect his teachers, perhaps particularly his new ones, to be courteous enough not to embarrass him by pointing out what may or may not actually be a shortcoming. How would a teacher like a little snip in one of his classes to try to disconcert him because of what that student sees as a failing?

Knowingly or unknowingly, a teacher will almost certainly provoke an administrator if the teacher says or implies that the administrator is doing his job improperly or that he must do something. No bosses anywhere need brook that kind of criticism from subordinates. A typical example happened in our school one year when three new and well-qualified members of our staff were competing for a single position the following year. At that time positions generally were difficult to secure. The teacher who in some ways was best qualified for the job went to her immediate supervisor, the person primarily responsible for deciding who of the three would be reappointed. She told him that it was getting late. (Wouldn't he have known that it was mid-March?) She also stated that he was "bound" to decide among the three at once so that the two who were not to be rehired could begin looking for other positions.

Examine the situation a little from her administrator's point of view. The three were entirely free to seek new work without knowing the fate of their current contracts. Further, how was her supervisor bound? He was not legally bound. The state date for notification of termination of contracts was over a month away. Was he morally bound? If anything, he was committed to the Board of Education to secure the best teacher possible, and given his buyer's market, he may have wished evidence from another month's classes before making his decision. Whatever his thinking, he did not answer her then but a month later with a letter indicating that she had been "a wonderful addition to the staff, but. . . ." Most likely she had reasoned that she was the best person for the job and that consequently she could pressure this administrator into giving her the position early. What she apparently failed to understand was that many factors, not merely or even primarily teaching ability, determine who gets a job. For one, an administrator must sense that he can work comfortably with the applicant. When this teacher approached her supervisor, he was wavering about which person to retain. Her directives helped him decide, even though she left our school convinced she had done the right thing.

What a person is really saying when he tries to tell his boss what to do is, "I am more capable than you, so let me tell you how to do your job or, better still, do it for you." The folly of such a tactic is so clear that most people don't need to be reminded to avoid it. Sometimes, however, instead of saying this, one implies it. Because that maneuver is a little more subtle, it usually is a little more deadly.

An instance of the latter revolved around an essay written by a junior and entitled, "On Literature." Everyone from Homer to Dostoevski to Joyce, as well as numerous American giants, was mentioned. The English teacher considered the paper name-dropping and pompous critical cant. Even so, the words were strung together well, and mechanically the paper was virtually errorless. The teacher decided to question the student about the writers mentioned, thereby revealing to him his inadequacy to attempt the subject, and then ask him to write another essay on a more specific and suitable topic. Before doing this, the teacher wanted confirmation that she was approaching the matter sensibly. She took the paper to her immediate supervisor and, without telling him what she thought of it, she asked him to read it and tell her his opinion. He thought it was excellent. Had the teacher thanked him, left, and questioned the student as she had already decided to do, no harm would have come. She proceeded, though, to show this administrator various inadequacies in the paper to prove that she, not he, had evaluated it properly. His reasoning rather than the student's was thus scorned. She put the administrator on the spot unjustifiably when he was asked to read the paper once and quickly; she had thoroughly familiarized herself with it. Because educators are particularly sensitive about their intellects, such rudeness is not quickly forgotten. And an administrator has the power to come out ahead, irrespective of whether he or the teacher is right.

Administrators naturally regard inexperienced teachers as the pawns, the most dispensable figures, in their ranks. Any chess player knows that a pawn is virtually defenseless when it is advanced alone. It cannot hope to survive other pawns, let alone more powerful figures. By this analogy a new teacher realizes that he risks his job when he incites conflict with an administrator. Because I did not understand this simple point when I was a first-year teacher, the results were nearly disastrous for my career. My classroom performance as a new teacher was quite ordinary. The only way in which I was outstanding that year was that I challenged my principal over what now appears to me a rather foolish issue: whether I would give my "fair share" or, finally, any token contribution to the Delaware Valley United Fund. I say the issue was not truly important to me because I am unopposed theoretically to most charities.

In that school, it seemed, everyone contributed to the fund; our principal prided herself on 100 percent support from the staff. The amount designated as my share seemed high to me—that was the first year I had earned a livable salary—so I wrote out a check for a lesser figure and carried it off to school. As I was about to present my contribution, I overheard the principal badgering another, more timid, first-year teacher whose donation was also below what the principal expected. To this day, I can work up ire about "fair shares" because private charities are not taxes. But when I ripped up my check before my principal, I was saying nothing really about fair shares. Rather I was pronouncing, "You cannot tell me what to do." Little did I realize then that administrators *can* tell teachers to do many things, and usually we must do them or resign. Even though, as it rather surprisingly turned out, I did not lose my job over this conflict I rashly initiated, I did not have any more peace of mind while I remained on that staff. The energy I expended to stay composed while under that principal's constant fire sapped virtually all of my strength. Afterward I realized that as important as confronting an administrator may occasionally be, it's silly to do so unless the issue means as much as personal serenity or a job.

Unless teachers incite an administrator, they don't have to worry about seeing one in their classrooms very often. An administrator usually has more pressing matters to consider than individual classes. One time teachers do see the boss, though, is during evaluation, a situation often fraught with anxiety. Beginning teachers especially are apt to be tense on those days, since renewed contracts are dependent on good evaluations, and most beginners realize they haven't had time to learn the subject matter thoroughly. Although a considerate evaluator will announce his visits before he appears, that doesn't change the fact that the teacher is in a test condition. (Administrators deny this, of course.)

Luckily for teachers, evaluations are almost inevitably facilitated by student cooperation. Students respond well on these days even if they are lackadaisical most of the rest of the time. They know that it's their teacher's work that is being reviewed, but in a vague way they must also feel they're under examination. After all, a school official is in the room, and students too probably want to appear well before him. A good class will go out of its way to ensure its teacher's success, as one of my classes demonstrated several years ago. Class began that day at the usual 7:40, and at 7:45 we were joined by my departmental chairman. Most teen-agers are not fully awake at that hour of the morning: our discussion definitely limped. Because it did and because an evaluation was in progress, I became nervous and the atmosphere in the room soon became tense. All experienced teachers know that a troublesome tension must be dispelled before very much learning can occur. Knowing something, however, doesn't mean one can change it, and on that morning as much as I wanted to, I was unable to alter the stifling atmosphere. The students realized this. When at 8:00 we were joined by our principal, known by all to be a ham, one student took over and quipped, "But you promised us Robert Redford." Because we all—principal, chairman, students, and I—were taken by surprise, we forgot ourselves for a moment. Once the self-consciousness was gone, a better lesson ensued.

Another idea to keep in mind about evaluations is that there is no absolute standard of appraisal. Beginning teachers are notoriously difficult markers because they judge against an artificial standard. If any teacher judges himself against a measure of imagined perfection, he'll rightly understand that he falls far short of that. However, a competent evaluator does not compare a beginner with master teachers but with other beginners. Good evaluators know what can be accomplished in one year and what can't.

One beginning teacher was absolutely terrified when the superintendent suddenly popped into the room during a lesson on

Chaucer. The new teacher remembered that the superintendent had been an English major in college and assumed therefore he would automatically have at hand all of the facts about that writer's life and work. The teacher was afraid that he would confuse some date or character, thereby unmasking his ignorance before his superior. Were his worries actually justified, though? How many specific facts can any person recall about a subject he has studied as recently as the previous year? Ten or more years had elapsed since the superintendent in this example had studied Chaucer. Furthermore, that administrator did not prepare for the observation by memorizing details about the subject. When a teacher reviews the material carefully before an evaluation, he usually has the facts of the lesson much straighter than the evaluator does. Finally, slipping on a fact doesn't cost a career. The evaluator wants to know that a teacher is competent to present generally accepted and major concepts of a given subject. If a teacher doesn't know the centuries in which Chaucer lived, doesn't know something of what English was like then, doesn't know why Chaucer's tales still come alive for students in the twentieth century, the teacher might admit to his incompetence to teach Chaucer. But even as gross a mistake as confusing two of Chaucer's characters would probably be interpreted as human error.

When a teacher discusses his work with an evaluator, little is gained by announcing weaknesses. Maybe the evaluator hasn't noticed them, or maybe he doesn't consider them weaknesses. Anyway, he'll have enough ideas without a teacher supplying him with more. Some confessions are forthcoming out of a false notion that self-insight shows intelligence. Others arise out of guilt. Regardless, they are almost always ill-advised unless one is in church, on a couch, or with a confidant. It's wiser for a teacher to listen to the evaluator's ideas rather than to chatter about the issues himself. In one instance a teacher who was being evaluated felt quite concerned that he had failed to establish a composition folder for each student as the teacher thought the project had been prescribed. He was ready to admit to his superior what he considered his inadequacy and plead for leniency. Before he could speak, the supervisor approached him and praised his good work on the project. It doesn't always happen this way, but too much modesty is seldom applauded. More palatable is a teacher who can accept praise graciously and who, without bragging, can express confidence in his own work.

Obviously some evaluations are going to be inequitable. It may be simply that for whatever reason the responsible person doesn't like the individual under review. One case involved a beginner who felt he had been continually harassed by his principal for about three months before contract renewal. Some of his principal's actions before other staff members made it appear that the newcomer was personally offensive to her. Moreover, the principal was in his classroom every day, sometimes twice a day, but never for more than two or three minutes. Rather than truly observing and helping him while she was there, she always drew attention to herself, destroying whatever rapport might have existed between him and the students. If the lights were on, she turned them off; if the shades were up, she pulled them down, and so on. Finally she tormented him sufficiently to give him a case against her. When she suggested in April that he resign at the end of the year, he refused. He was not even sure then he wanted to continue teaching, but she had aroused him enough to want that decision to be his rather than hers. He insisted upon a review of his case by her superior. During a lengthy interview he convinced the latter that what the principal judged as his poor performance resulted in some measure from her mistreatment of him. His contract was renewed and he was transferred to another school within the district for the following year where, as it turned out, his work was judged excellent.

While this teacher handled his situation independently, in most schools today the best protection in cases like these is the teacher organization. It can interpret contractual rights, such as requisite number of evaluatory sessions and evaluators. It can also assist a teacher in establishing legally that his critique was unjust. The organization usually requests documentation to support charges. Copies of correspondence and evaluations are needed, and it is helpful as well if a teacher has kept a log or diary of incidents so that he can present his case specifically.

Although injustice sometimes arises, more usually an administrator hopes that persons he hires will become permanent members of the staff. Needless to say, time and money must be spent to train new teachers. An administrator normally determines during interviews that for his purposes a teacher knows enough about the subject to teach it. Relatively few contracts are withheld because of a lack of knowledge of subject; other matters are more important.

Setting aside reasons virtually beyond an administrator's control, such as budgetary reductions, why do teachers lose jobs? The chief reason is provoking an administrator personally. As already discussed, a personal affront to a superior is usually not forgotten. A second reason is a failure to carry out assigned duties. A teacher's most important obligation, first, last, and always, is to be with his classes at the scheduled times. If he leaves the classroom unattended for five minutes to go to the bathroom and one of the students injures another, the teacher is legally responsible. An administration is necessarily embarrassed when the staff is involved in litigation. Ironically, a teacher's actual success in the classroom is of less concern to anybody else than to the teacher himself. Only rarely are students, their parents, other teachers, or even supervisors driven to complain about a teacher's methods. He must, though, be in the classroom and manage his problems. The difficulty of the latter for a new teacher cannot be minimized, but no one, not an administrator nor a colleague, has time or inclination to do anyone else's job. Beyond classroom responsibilities, duties vary from school to school. However, knowing where an administration expects a teacher to be and what it expects him to do there, and then being there and doing it are essential for keeping a job. Usually doing more than what is expected is as little appreciated as doing less.

A third reason that contracts are not renewed is failure to become a cooperative member of a school's professional "team." Actually, much talk to the contrary, most teachers are not good team persons. They're star performers and often a little jealous about their arenas. To become an active and helpful member of an existing faculty, a new teacher must quickly and unobtrusively learn how to fit in.

Faculty

At the word "teacher," many people conjure up an image of a fairly intelligent person diligently working to improve his beloved students. As with any group, though, teachers come in all shapes and sizes. Some of them are intelligent; some almost stupid. Some are diligent; some lazy. Some love kids, even to the point of indulging them; others are almost sadistic. Most teachers fall somewhere between these extremes.

A new teacher becomes acquainted with this potpourri formally at faculty meetings and informally in faculty lounges or, in large schools, in departmental offices. The types are predictable. There's the chronic complainer: school rules aren't clear. He offers no solutions, but disaster is always impending. There's the pedant: school rules aren't clear, and he knows just the comma that produces the ambiguity. There's the scholar: school rules aren't clear, as we could have foreseen had we been aware of their historical antecedents. There's the cynic: of course school rules aren't clear. Fools make them up and only fools follow them. There's the peacemaker: school rules aren't clear, but we must all cheerfully work together anyway. Finally, when we're lucky, there's the clown: thank goodness school rules aren't clear. If they were, we might have to follow them. Most teachers love to hear themselves talk.

Not as immediately recognizable as types, but more important to survival in a school, is the pecking order of a faculty. Actually, each separate group of employees, including the administration, has its own hierarchy, and in large schools there is also a hierarchy within the staff of each department. Often at meetings the people who are really in charge don't speak, or they don't speak much. There're several ways, though, of discerning faculty leaders. One is to observe who associates frequently and informally with the principal or other officials. Another indication of leadership is repeated appointment or election to prestigious commit-tees. Still another sign is the ability to have the last word in a faculty room argument. Usually VIPs are too busy to notice first-year teachers very much, but it never hurts to know on whom one can peck. Although we might like to think differently, schools are not exempt from practical politics. When annoyed, influen-tial faculty members may try to sway administrators about an individual's assignments or even about his position on the staff. The interesting thing is that this almost always happens behind the back of the teacher concerned; all of a sudden he finds him-self with assignments nobody wants. If it comes down to where he's actually dismissed or asked to resign, all he will be told is that he wasn't doing his job well enough. The charge that he provoked someone on the staff just wouldn't stand up, would it?

One of the occupational hazards of teaching is fault-finding. In a teacher's zeal to help students improve, he shows them their errors. If this habit carries over into his relationships with adults, he is in trouble since no one appreciates having his own short-comings discussed by anybody else. Only an unprofessional teach-er discusses colleagues in any way with students, only a gossip maliciously berates one coworker to another, and only a sneak informs on a coworker to a superior. No teacher is responsible for his colleagues' shortcomings; he can do nothing about them; he can only be happy if he doesn't suffer from the same problems.

Naturally, anybody with a mind to can observe the numerous peccadilloes of any staff: one teacher is always late to class; an-other doesn't mark his papers; one always leaves early; one is having an affair with another teacher—or with a student, for that matter. The list is endless, as it would be with any group of people. This much is certain too: secrets are almost impossible to keep in a school. If a teacher notices a fault of a colleague, it's safe to assume that administrators know about that inadequacy also. They may not act because of long years of service or because of difficulty of proof. Take an instance of nervous exhaustion (and a year or two of classroom combat convinces any teacher that this is something to which he's prone), the proof of inability to perform because of fatigue might become almost impossible to establish.

Many years ago I was a secretary at a school in which one of the teachers was an alcoholic. His excesses were so flagrant that I wondered why something wasn't done. Apparently, though, there were at least two reasons why he wasn't asked to resign. First, his family was influential in that town. Second, although the school knew of his intoxication on duty, the community at large did not. The situation had gone on for several years, and to dismiss him would have looked bad for the school as well as for the individual. Administrators usually try to avoid airing internal problems publicly.

That case brings to mind another, much less serious one involving alcohol. As is common, a rule in one school stated that there were to be no alcoholic beverages on campus. One day, though, a teacher noticed unopened beer cans in the supply closet of one classroom. Although he was assigned to that room for only one period, he could have been accused of bringing the beer to class. It was not really his place to remove the cans, and to confront his colleague who also taught in the room could easily have blown the incident out of proportion. Rather as soon as he could, he described the situation to his immediate supervisor. What happened after that was up to the supervisor, not the teacher. The teacher wasn't trying to be the hand of justice. He simply didn't want to be blamed for something that wasn't his fault.

Teachers are, at times, unfeeling toward one another. Often it's a matter of getting up on the wrong side of the bed and snapping at a colleague. Or maybe a teacher retaliates in kind when he thinks a colleague has wronged him. Occasionally one teacher will spite another for personal advancement. Suppose older teachers test a beginner. They may want to discover what he's like before admitting him to their circle. Once in a discussion on the Civil War, an old-timer suggested that a new teacher's ideas must have come from an eighth-grade textbook. How is a new teacher to respond to a colleague's implication that she's fairly ignorant and unsophisticated? Is she to retort angrily? Is she to shut up meekly? That newcomer had gumption enough to remain unruffled and to continue to contribute her point of view.

Rarely do beginners make themselves objectionable enough to the established staff to provoke genuine antipathies. It is true that some older staff members are envious of the freshness and youth of new teachers, but most aren't. They remember the difficulties of beginning and are only too thankful for their age and experience. Importantly, a beginner is different from veteran teachers in several ways, and to the extent that those differences become threatening, he will be disagreeable to them. The speech and dress of a new teacher, two of the first things noticed about any person, are usually less conservative than that of his colleagues simply because he's younger. His conversation will contain some of the hip jargon of his high school and college years; many of those words his new peers may not even know. Moreover, a twenty-two-year-old just out of college will find that his clothes more closely resemble those of his seventeen- and eighteen-year-old students than they do those of even his thirty-five- and forty-year-old colleagues, not to mention those of older ones. Although advertisements convince many of us that a youthful look is *the* desirable look, once over forty we can't achieve that look no matter how we try to assist nature. Even the slightest hint of our inability from someone who has naturally what we want is somewhat disconcerting.

One day a new teacher with a shock of naturally wavy blond hair bemoaned the fact that he had to allow ten minutes each morning after his shower to blow his hair dry and style it. Most of us sympathized with that daily curtailment of sleep. Then he turned to an older man, who achieved his full-shock look with a full wig. All the newcomer said was, "You're lucky you don't have such problems." But implicit in his remark was, one, that the wig was obvious and, two, that his colleague's age was showing. An isolated slip like this would almost certainly be overlooked, but a consistent callousness of this type would indicate an insensitivity toward older workers.

Experienced teachers see the school and teaching somewhat differently from beginners simply because experienced teachers have been around longer and have more of a vested interest in the place. Contrary to what a beginner might expect, most experienced teachers don't like to hear constant raves about wonderful "new" teaching methods; it doesn't matter either if those methods were learned at Podunk U. or at Harvard U. To survive, teachers settle into a routine in which each class period is no longer a crisis. Most of them have no desire to change their teaching methods, and most of them couldn't even if they wanted to. It's irritating, therefore, for them to be told that their methods are second-best, or even to have it implied that they are, especially when the instruction comes from an inexperienced person. Experienced teachers have to accept criticisms from superiors, from students, and from students' parents. They don't have to listen to them from new teachers.

Another difference between inexperienced and "seasoned" teachers is that many of the latter have lost some of their idealism. At first it may shock a beginner to hear an older teacher say, "Oh, there's nothing to be done for that student; he's absolutely incorrigible." The beginner has probably been taught that no student is unreachable; it is the duty of a teacher to find just the right way. Another veteran may declare, "Of course twenty-minute periods aren't educationally sound, but there's nothing teachers can do to change that." Most likely the novice has been taught that it is the responsibility of all teachers to work to change weaknesses in a school. Rightly or wrongly, previous frustrations in trying to effect change often cause teachers to see such effort as futile. They believe, though, that they are subsequently more realistic rather than less idealistic. Furthermore, most teachers I have known are altogether convinced about the difference an education can make in a person's life, and to that extent they remain idealistic. Older teachers tend to "forgive" beginners their more intense idealism, remembering a similar phase in their own careers. What they don't look on very kindly is an inference by a new teacher that they are somehow bad or wrong if their ideas of what it is possible to accomplish in teaching have changed over the years.

Teaching often entails numerous hardships: crowded schedules, extra duties, cramped teaching posts, wretched students. The list could go on ad infinitum. Well mindful of seniority on a staff, veteran teachers expect the best schedules, rooms, supplies, and students to be parceled out to themselves. Occasionally administrators try to ease a beginner's situation in these regards, but more usually he should accept the least desirable assignments and physical conditions graciously. Chronic complaints about a school from an individual who has just joined a faculty are like chronic criticisms about a family from someone who has recently married into it. The newcomer just shouldn't make them because he's still an outsider. Anyway, complaining at any time is suggestive of whining, an unpleasant attitude at best.

Although a new teacher will most likely have to swallow some disagreeable working conditions, he doesn't have to accept passively true injustice from colleagues. The best place to remedy problems like these is at the source of the trouble, if happily that source is known. Say an older teacher keeps coming into a beginner's room, ostensibly to get supplies. If the older teacher seems to have motives beyond his obvious ones, there is no reason why he should not be asked to stop. If he persists, the next step for the new teacher is to discuss the situation with his immediate supervisor. Teachers are not hired to supervise each other, and a new teacher need not be subjected to such "help," especially if he thinks it prevents him from doing his job well. The less commotion made, though, the better, and the less help required to solve the conflict the better.

Frequently new teachers may feel that they don't know how they're going to get through the next school hour, let alone the next day or the next week. One such newcomer on our staff met her Waterloo by convincing everyone that she couldn't do her job. After enlisting our help for making up lesson plans and assignments, she worried that those plans were incomplete. Next she fretted that she did not know enough to teach her students because they were so bright—she as much as told the students this too, a fatal error. Finally, she sobbed that her classes didn't respect her. How could they have after she had told them she couldn't teach them? Perhaps she was misguided into thinking that others would help her deny her inability once she unabashedly admitted it. Some of the kinder ones among us listened patiently and tried to help, but most simply considered her rather foolish.

In comparison to a beginner's plight, veterans on a staff may appear to have everything under control. They don't. I was astounded the first year I taught to hear a very experienced teacher say that he didn't know what he was going to do with his tenth-period class. The students were loud, obnoxious, ignorant, and totally uninterested in his biology lessons. Moreover, from the looks of things in another room opposite my hall duty post that year, the students were going wild for about the first six weeks of school. That teacher had been publicly praised as "terrific," yet he obviously wasn't, at least not in the beginning of the year. Of course, experienced teachers usually do have more successes than failures, and merely by listening in the faculty room, many of their secrets can be divined. Listening and observing, moreover, are always preferable to asking, regardless of what administrators might suggest during orientation. Most experienced staffers really don't want a beginning teacher added to their list of pupils. Essentially, they must become convinced that a new teacher will be a pleasant coworker.

Special Services

As the affluence of a community increases, so too do its school specialists, now commonly including librarians, counselors, psychologists, social workers, and nurses. Usually the image of a staff projected to outsiders or new personnel is that of one big happy family eager to serve students. Anyone who comes from a large family, though, knows that size as often gives rise to strife as to bliss. Although most of these specialists do want to serve students, they may disagree with teachers about how best to accomplish this. Furthermore, a teacher usually feels that in its scheduled time his class is a student's most important responsibility, but specialists have the prerogative of calling any student from a class. They, too, have to work during school hours because that's the only time students are available to them.

Somewhat surprisingly, open conflicts on a staff are much less frequent and annoying than they might be simply because, except for guidance counselors, teachers don't work very closely with most of these specialists. Happy to accept their various services, teachers also have to accept each group's own procedures, determined by the hierarchy within that group and by administrative directives. Teachers, for instance, might conceive of high school libraries as work areas in which absolute silence is neither feasible nor desirable. Unless, however, the librarians and administrators see the function of the library in the same way, the library will be quiet—that is, as quiet as any high school library can ever be.

Teachers are encouraged to cooperate with guidance counselors if a student's performance is at all unusual. Teachers may share responsibility with psychologists, social workers, and nurses as well, but not with the regularity with which they must join counselors. A guidance counselor is a liaison between home and school if things aren't going well for a student. Depending upon a counselor's time and talent, he may also help a student select his high-school courses and his college, counsel him personally and vocationally, and even discipline him if school rules so provide.

Because of all these functions, guidance counselors like to say that it is they who know the "whole" student, whereas his teachers see him only as a math student, a history student, or an English student. Teachers, though, feel that guidance counselors can't know the whole student either: counselors see students individually, while teachers have to be concerned about how they behave in class. Therefore, unhealthy competition sometimes arises between a guidance counselor and a teacher about who knows what's best for a student, who cares more about him, and who works harder for him. Students seem aware of such antagonism, even though it's seldom spoken of openly, and they often pit their counselors and teachers against each other in order to achieve what they themselves want. Let's say a student wants to be transferred from one section of math to another because his best friend is in the other section. School rules require legitimate reasons for transfers, and this student knows that wanting to be with his friend won't pass muster. However, if he can convince his counselor that his current teacher picks on him or that the class is really too difficult for him, he has a good chance to be moved. In another instance a student may realize that even though it is too late in the year to transfer, he is doing quite poorly in a class. He may be able to persuade his counselor to intercede with his teacher for him. Teachers often find counselors reminding them of the ill effects of failure on a student and pointing out various emotional and physical problems contributing to the student's failure. Their diagnosis of his predicament seldom seems to include laziness.

A school is strengthened if its staff has genuine philosophical discussion about the causes of academic success and failure, but it is never aided by in-staff backbiting. Because most of us know this, the usual solution is that both guidance counselors and teachers learn rather quickly each other's characters and reputations. (There are both strict and lenient members in each group.) These judgments help them determine whom they can work with. If a teacher is having a problem with a student and thinks that consultation with a guidance counselor will help to solve the problem, the teacher seeks that help. By the same token, if at all possible he will avoid those counselors with whom he feels he cannot work. I am certain the reverse also holds true.

Nonprofessional Staff

Anyone who thinks that only the professionals in a school know and decide what goes on in a building is poorly informed. Nonprofessional workers, including cooks and bus drivers, but especially secretaries and janitors, contribute significantly. They may go anywhere in a building at almost any time, whereas teachers usually carry keys only for those rooms in which they work. Nonprofessionals may interrupt classes with messages and supplies. Janitors may "observe" teachers while they make repairs in rooms. Further, they can interpret what goes on in rooms in a less obvious way: they see the trash. If a party takes place in a classroom (parties are often forbidden in high schools), the janitors will know it. Secretaries are privy to virtually any file in a building, whether of staff or of students, whereas teachers lack such access. Teachers usually must obtain information about students from guidance counselors or administrators. Often a secretary is also the confidante of her boss and thus privileged to know many school secrets. There's an old saying that actually the janitors and secretaries run a school. Those of us who laugh at this probably do so because we understand its truth.

A summer school teacher once saw an advantage in moving a class from its scheduled room to a larger and cooler one. Because the second room was not scheduled to be used, the principal agreed that a change should be effected. On Friday the class moved into the new room. The custodian, however, found problems with this change; the move would necessitate additional work by his men. On Monday the principal told the teacher to return to his original room. The reasons remained unexplained to the teacher, but the larger and cooler room remained vacant essentially because the janitor had decreed that it should.

Since new teachers are at the bottom of the instructional staff, they occasionally are tempted to think that they can at least lord it over janitors and secretaries. Those workers do serve teachers by the very nature of their jobs, while the reverse is not true. However, janitors and secretaries may well have some privileges teachers do not. One new teacher was irate when he discovered that a janitor had been assigned a choice parking space. The teacher had been told that because of insufficient places he would have to fend for himself on the streets. Simply put, the janitor had seniority.

Most nonprofessional workers in a school will not take orders from a teacher. They have supervisors to direct them. If they fail to do something, and this omission affects the way a teacher can do his job, the teacher's only recourse may be to go through proper channels. A teacher in a large school, for instance, found that her floor badly needed mopping, since there had been several days of particularly inclement weather. Suggestions to the janitor that he might do this produced only a smile because that wasn't the week to mop floors. The teacher then requested the cleaning through her immediate supervisor, who in turn passed her request along to the head janitor, who in turn told the janitor to mop the floor, who in turn did it. These circuitous strategies may seem foolish at first, but, after all, I probably would not listen to a janitor who told me to unlock my room each morning at 7:30 so that early students could enter. I would accept the same directive from my principal without question, provided that hour was part of our contractual agreement.

Teachers do not like to do the work of other employees; the opposite is equally true. Asking a secretary or a janitor to do a teacher's job may be bluntly or hostilely refused. When teachers do find themselves dependent on these fellow workers for personal favors, a remuneration usually makes the request more palatable. If I wanted a janitor to water the plants in my room during a vacation, for example, I would expect to reimburse him for his additional work. Secretaries and janitors work more weeks of the year for considerably less money than teachers do. While differences in training and responsibilities justify this variance, it may not always be justified in these other workers' minds, especially if teachers try to take exceptions to the rules by which all must be governed or if they try to pawn off some of their work on others.

All workers in a school have a time schedule to follow, even though some teachers are persuaded that the schedule of other workers is less important than theirs. It may annoy a teacher, for instance, that a janitor insists on sweeping a classroom after school at the same time the teacher is giving a make-up test in it. The teacher is concerned that the distraction may interfere with students' work. He can't understand why the janitor can't sweep another room and return to his later. The janitor, though, has his routine too and if a particular room isn't swept, the teacher is probably the first to complain. At other times teachers are irked that secretaries forever seem to have something for them to do: complete these forms, hand in grades, give an assignment for Johnny who's been sick this week—and do all these things before 3:00 P.M. How, a teacher may argue, can they expect me to act on such ridiculously short notice? How can they expect me to do these things in addition to everything else I'm supposed to do? Secretaries, though, are only enunciating their bosses' directives and in doing so often incur rebukes really meant for, but judiciously not given to, administrators.

At one level the perspectives of all workers in a school are limited: a janitor knows that his year must consist of so many desks straightened and so many floors swept; a secretary's year must include so many stencils typed and forms completed; a teacher's, so many classes taught and papers marked. Any job reduced to its mechanics soon becomes tedious and meaningless. At the same time we can never totally forget these duties, because they occupy so much of our lives. Naturally we all appreciate someone showing that he understands our particular point of view.

New teachers are sometimes advised to "cultivate" friendships with custodians and secretaries in order to facilitate their own work. Shunning such a despicable tactic does not mean that they should avoid these coworkers. At one school I was greeted daily by a man about five-two, pushing a broom, who said, "Good mornin', darlin'. How're you today? You're certainly lookin' gorgeous." This rogue did not single out any one woman for his endearments: we were all his darlings—students, teachers, guidance counselors, whoever, as long as we accepted his playful teasing. Like many others, I came to look forward to his perpetual cheerfulness and reassurance. Often one of my favorite moments of the day now is when another janitor comes to empty the wastebasket in my office. This man readily discusses everything from the weather to Carlton Fredericks to medicine to flowers, and his stories are captivating once he starts. Without exploitation teachers naturally benefit from the services of fellow workers, as well as from their wit and wisdom.

These pages have made so little of friendly camaraderie among staff members that a wary beginner may wonder if no one at his new job will welcome him. Of course they will! With but one exception the atmosphere of all schools in which I have worked has been filled with friendliness and cooperation. New teachers may even be wined and dined at first. As a year progresses, new teachers and experienced teachers naturally share many pleasures and frustrations. Nevertheless, from my observations any proffers of true friendship extended toward first-year teachers have been as infrequent as any genuine ill will directed at them. New teachers often find themselves left alone much more than they had expected to be. The beginning of a career is an incredible step to a beginner himself; for the first time he has not just a job but a salaried position. Experienced workers, though, are not particularly dazzled that someone else has completed his formal education and started to work. They are comfortably settled with their colleagues and students. Whether a new teacher can find a place among them is largely his unaided task.

VI
Goals of Education

Before the teacher could finish returning the graded essays, one of the brightest students in the class exploded, "How can you give me a B? Your only criticism of my analysis is its length, but I did more, not less, than what was expected." His teacher continued to hand other students their papers, trying to ignore the boy's heated consultations with classmates around him. Did they think, he wanted to know, that the teacher had been fair? The teacher recalled the day he had assigned the 500-word essay. Most students had groaned they'd never be able to write that much. A few, though, including the presently outspoken boy, had asked if it would be permissible to write more than that. While the teacher had agreed he wouldn't count off for 498 or 502 words, he had clearly indicated that the limit was 500. Now that this student was upset, however, the teacher began to wonder if he had done the right thing.

A teacher's uncertainty about what to do in a situation like this often reflects that he isn't clear about the very goals of education. Had he thought that strict adherence to the 500-word limit would have educational value? This issue is subordinate to a more general question: exactly what do we mean when we regard someone as educated? Is mere possession of information or skills commensurate with being educated? If not, what else is needed? A teacher who can answer questions like these can confidently determine what and how he should teach.

Goal 1: Information

An educated person must have information about place, time, environment, numbers, and words. In school it was my fourth-grade teacher who introduced me to a study of place. I still remember marveling at the exotic sounds of "Tigris" and "Euphrates" and "Mesopotamia" in that book labeled *World Geography*. But though the names captivated, the course left me with the impression that geography was somehow remote and impractical. I did not realize that when my father had earlier taught me that our barn was west of our house I had also learned geography. No matter where we want to go, we realize the usefulness of orientation in space, which begins with a child's learning his home address and ends with a knowledge of world geography.

In addition, this subject is absorbing. If no one except an airplane navigator needs to know whether Chicago is directly west, northwest, or southwest of New York City, the answer is still intriguing. Equally engrossing is why the Norfolk Island pine, now a popular house plant in the United States, has its growing season in winter. Most people derive personal satisfaction from understanding how our globe is organized, even though its political organization changes from time to time. When I went to school the only names one really had to associate with Africa were Egypt, the Belgian Congo, and South Africa. Today anyone limited to that list is as naïve as a person who imagines that a sheik still travels on a camel instead of in his private limousine or jet.

In most American schools today geography is hidden in a course called social studies. The thinking is that geographic data will be more meaningful if it is learned along with historic and other social information. While this idea may be true, what often happens is that geography is relegated to a position of second- or third-rank importance. Furthermore, since most American high school students learn primarily American history and hence American geography, they are usually woefully uninformed about world geography. Most would be unable to answer even elementary questions like these: What is the capital of Hungary? In what country is Buenos Aires? Where is Latvia?

In addition to knowing about place, an educated person must also have a perspective of time. Best acquired through a study of history, such perception is difficult to develop and is dependent somewhat upon a person's own age. A small child who has just celebrated a birthday has no clear understanding how long he will have to wait for another anniversary. A year is an eon to him. When we were about eight, my best friend and I asked her mother how old she was. We were amazed to learn that somebody could actually be thirty-six. Now that I am forty-two, that incident seems funny, and yet I cannot think how I will perceive the world when I am, say, ninety. I cannot truly imagine how my aunt, who is that age, conceives of past or future. She was a little girl during the Spanish-American War, while to me that war will always belong to the unknown past. Moreover, what does she anticipate in death? We are as baffled by the length of eternity as a child is by the length of the next year.

If asked what is meant by the study of history, most students would respond with a few political names and dates. Those are essential; think of the history of Europe without milestones like 1066, 1789, and 1918. However, equally as decisive for an understanding of that continent during this 850-year period were the invention of the printing press, Newton's statement of the laws of physics and the discovery of electricity. Many would be hard pressed to suggest even the century of these happenings. Ideally history should include the political, social, economic, intellectual, and artistic life of a country studied chronologically. Often a single issue has ramifications in all of these areas. Any country's history is also tied intimately to that of the rest of the world. Although we take this for granted when we approach current events, it is frequently ignored when we examine the past.

I was a history major in college, and yet when I graduated if someone had asked me why it was important to study history, all I could have answered was that one studied history to learn about the past. I really hadn't the foggiest notion why anyone should want to learn about the past. I wonder now whether all of my professors themselves had a clear idea on this. If they did, they certainly didn't convey it to us. Consequently, the information we gathered was meaningful primarily because it allowed us to pass examinations.

Many years went by before I understood that the greatest benefit of studying history might be the objectivity it gives one about his own time. Without a knowledge of history, a person is apt to condescend toward times past, thinking that because his age appears different, it is improved. When my students read plays or novels from earlier centuries, their first reaction is often, "We're not like that anymore." This is what they almost invariably claim, for instance, when they begin to discuss Ibsen's *A Doll's House*. They insist that no modern woman would stoop to lie to her husband about something as trivial as eating macaroons. She'd tell him it was none of his concern what she ate. My students soon admit, though, that even a modern working woman might very well tell her husband she paid less for a dress than she did if she thought that was the only way to keep peace and have the dress at the same time. A little such probing helps them realize that deceitful wives like Nora and possessive, domineering husbands like Torvald are very much a part of our contemporary scene. If we modernized the clothes and speech of these characters, we could watch them almost any night on television.

Apparently, only the outward trappings of times change; the aspirations and fears of people remain fairly constant through the ages. Isn't this why we still have wars, even though people acknowledge that those conflicts are deplorable? The pecking order must be maintained, whether on the personal level of the family or on the global level of nations. No sacrifice is too large for that, and each party in a conflict believes it has no alternative but to fight. That human motivation is largely unchanging explains why we are horrified or delighted, as the case warrants, by the stories of history; they concern us as much as they did persons of earlier times. In this way we also gain an increased perception of the achievements and errors of our time, even if we cannot expect knowledge of past events to prevent us from repeating earlier mistakes. Correction, after all, is a matter of character or perhaps destiny as much as it is of information.

There are valid reasons for approaching almost any academic discipline historically. This approach to the study of environment, the subject matter of science, would surely enhance our understanding of scientific information currently held to be true. People of any age tend to believe that the scientists of their era speak immutable truth. We find it difficult now to believe that persons several centuries ago put their faith in bloodletting as a curative. But in another hundred years or so persons will undoubtedly question in the same way what to them are the backward techniques of the twentieth century. We already regard with horror the electric shock treatments and lobotomies regularly performed as "cures" for mental patients less than a quarter century ago. Moreover, if scientific judgment is always accurate, why is it that there are frequent scientific controversies, such as the current dispute about vitamins? Some authorities hold that a person who eats a balanced diet doesn't need to take vitamin supplements, that excess vitamins consumed are merely excreted. Others make various claims for ingesting these tablets, including the idea that vitamin C not only cures the common cold and cancer but also prolongs life. Students should be taught to question scientific information even though they must look to science to provide them with important information about self and environment.

Because scientists frequently use mathematics in their work and because of the objectivity associated with these two disciplines, it's not surprising that mathematics is often considered a science. Science, though, is either an objective description of physical phenomena (descriptive science), or it is a method for studying cause-and-effect relationships (experimental science). Sometimes people erroneously equate science with a particular subject rather than with a method of study. To them only subjects like physics or chemistry or biology can represent scientific knowledge. They laugh at the idea of political science because they don't see how material as unpredictable as human nature can be approached with scientific objectivity. However, almost any discipline can be studied scientifically if an experiment is designed stating the cause and the effect to be tested and explaining the method of the test so that it can be duplicated and its conclusion verified.

Mathematics, on the other hand, develops methods for problem solving with various practical and theoretical applications. It employs its own language, one that is more precise and objective than other languages. For that reason mathematics is especially helpful in understanding the world in which we live. Einstein's famous $E = mc^2$ demonstrates how closely math is allied to science, even though their methods are different. Einstein devised the way whereby he could provide a mathematical proof for this equation, which expresses his conception of the universe. An experimental scientist accepts mathematical proofs only as suggestions that have to be validated experimentally. This is a point at which science and math go separate ways.

The importance of mathematics in education is undisputed. Even time and distance are predicated numerically, and a person who lacks skill in arithmetic is severely handicapped. Besides its practical uses, problem solving is intriguing. A tangential benefit associated with the study of mathematics is the development of logical reasoning. Although many other disciplines seek to develop this faculty, illogic is easier to detect in mathematics than, say, in a paragraph of historical argument. Many of our generalizations about persons and nationalities exist because we don't scrutinize the generalizations logically. This is why the little boy can think that because his sister is mean all other women are mean as well. Many adults who snicker about that illogic can still be heard to say that southerners are slow, that Poles are stupid, that Japanese are polite. . . .

The extent of a person's education is often said to be revealed as soon as he speaks. This would explain why many people quiver when they discover they're in the presence of an English teacher. Many times they excuse themselves by promising to watch their language. When I hear such apologies, I'm always tempted to answer, "Well, if you want to speak correctly, speak like I do." The joke, though, would probably be lost on anyone worried about his speech. Errors in language do show a great deal about people. Take a common error such as, "They wanted Jane and I to go." Stemming as it does from overcorrection, the form suggests that a person may lack intelligence to apply what he has learned about the cases of pronouns or that he may be too lazy to do so. He may also err in language if he is a victim of his environment or if he resists the implicit snobbery underlying considerations of correctness.

What is "correct" in any language is nothing more or less than a social consideration. There is no self-evident reason, for instance, why the verb "ain't" is nonstandard; a number of centuries ago that form was the standard contraction for "am not," "are not," and "is not." Today, however, "ain't" is associated with the speech of persons who have little schooling. Who decides these matters is none other than the educated folk themselves, influenced by the tastes of persons in the social register. Using what these groups determine to be the standard forms of a language does nothing to improve a person's communication, but it may open—or close—certain business or social doors for him.

In some circles a scant vocabulary marks one as uneducated. It doesn't matter whether a person is lazy or doesn't care; if he has to rely on one word to express many different ideas, he is limited. Suppose, for instance, that someone said he had a *nice* time on a *nice* day after he met a *nice* person. A friend of mine trying to establish the adequacy of her vocabulary once informed me that she had filled out her reports "metriculously." Such amusing conglomerates can result because people confuse "big" with "better." Others use words imprecisely because they don't really think about what they say; they just talk. Students should be taught that an educated person not only has an adequate number of words at his disposal, but also he takes pleasure in using those words precisely.

Language is vital to all other areas of education, even though originally a child learns a great deal about place, time, environment, and probably about numbers without language. The child is pleased, though, to learn words because they help him express his discovery of his world and of himself. If he is told that "moon" is the word for the ball in the sky, that word can help him tell others about his find. From the infant to the most erudite of scholars, the give and take of information is immeasurably enhanced by the symbols of language. The more complex the matter, the greater necessity that the language be exact. For this reason every educated person is expected to know his own language well. Besides this, knowledge of another language should increase one's power of communication because he sees that the same thing can be said another way.

Most people, of course, look to schools to acquaint them with these areas of information requisite for education. Since this is so, many ask, Why don't schools do a better job? Why do so many students graduate knowing as little as they do? Critics rail about poor instruction and poor motivation. They often fail to admit that a part of the problem is the fault neither of teachers nor of students.

Teachers in schools have traditionally had to rely too much on books and too little on experience. Anyone who tries to read a "how to" book finds that a great part of the information is lost until he himself actually tries to perform. Consider a schoolboy studying a foreign language from books. He can never be as motivated to speak that language as will an immigrant trying to communicate with those in his new country. The immigrant is at a disadvantage too if he must learn the language without proper instruction or books. He is unable to judge whether the speech he is imitating is the speech generally considered acceptable. While a combination of books and experience is acknowledged as the best teacher, experience is often too time-consuming and costly for schools to provide. Relying on books alone, students find much information stale.

Another reason students find some information difficult to absorb is that they personally aren't old enough to relate it to their lives. A great deal can be said for the old idea that "education is wasted on the young," even though societies have persistently made youth the time for concentrated study. When I was in third grade I resisted learning multiplication tables. Since my buying then was limited to an occasional candy bar or ice-cream cone, I couldn't really understand why I needed to be able to multiply. I also fought practicing the piano at about that age. How could I have been expected to grasp the idea that those lessons were meant to instill self-discipline as much as they were intended to improve my musical technique? In any subject much of what is regarded as useful or important is useful or important from an adult's point of view.

Many of the events and concepts of history, as well as the themes of art, are based on adult emotions and experiences. Lacking firsthand understanding of those, a person is usually powerless to comprehend fully the material that schools nevertheless have the responsibility of introducing to him. The point is illustrated well by Arthur Miller's *Death of a Salesman,* a work widely taught in high schools. Miller pictures the younger son as doomed to repeat the mistakes of his father's tragic life. Most high school students, though, support the son's own naïve conclusion that he can make his fortune and still have spiritual independence. Because students themselves have not experienced the difficulty of that maneuver, they reject what the play subtly shows them about it. This gap between a reader's life and a book explains why many people, upon rereading a work they first encountered in high school, exclaim, "Oh, is that what that book meant?"

Actually most of us find ourselves in later years seeking out information we earlier were exposed to but somehow didn't absorb. Some even think that we are all doomed to die uneducated. That is true, though, only if we mean that there will always be more information for us to learn. And what does it matter finally that a person can spout off names, dates, and ideas as if he were an encyclopedia? Information per se is meaningless. Unless a person's character and his enjoyment of life are enhanced by what he knows, the knowledge is of no true avail to him. Incidentally, we put our youth to school rather than our middle-aged or elderly because a child's character can be molded by the information received and by the process of learning itself.

Goal 2: Expanded Range of Interests

Imagine a person with very little education. What are his interests? If we ask a small child what he wants to be when he grows up, his choice is usually restricted to his father's occupation or to neighborhood jobs that appear glamorous to him, such as those of firemen and policemen. He likes to eat only those foods he is accustomed to and in the way his mother prepares them. If we ask him whether he would like to hear a story and allow him to select a book, he will normally hand us a well-worn volume. His selection in all of these areas, as well as others, is limited.

Even though adults with little education might agree that variety is stimulating, they are more or less restricted to the tastes and interests they acquired as children. They don't like to try anything new because it seems strange. A person who has grown up with only country and western songs is not going to like Bach's music the first time he hears it. (This is not snobbery; a person used to hearing only Bach will not enjoy Tchaikovsky the first time either.) Suppose, however, we increase the range slightly so that a person likes hymns and jazz in addition to country music. He too may not like Bach initially, but he will be less likely to reject him as quickly as the person who knows only one kind of music. The difference is his knowledge that various types of music may give him pleasure. Usually the more varied a person's experience, the less resistant he will be to experiment with something new. He knows little is lost if he ultimately doesn't like it, and he also realizes that it's foolish to reject something merely because he doesn't like it initially. Many tastes from foods to arts are slowly acquired. And if a person ultimately decides that he likes, for example, country and western best, his preference has been established by independent selection. He's not stuck with country and western simply because of lack of experience.

One of the best means by which a teacher can encourage his

students to expand their range of interests is to introduce new material enthusiastically. This is not the same as telling them why they're supposed to like a particular subject or why it will be good for them to know it, but rather conveying exactly why the subject appeals to the teacher personally. The catch is genuineness. A teacher can't project true enthusiasm unless he feels it, and there is always plenty about any subject that won't kindle anybody's ardor. As an example, I taught Emily Dickinson's "A Narrow Fellow in the Grass" for a number of years before I truly appreciated the poem myself. It took a personal experience, finally, to convince me of the perfection of the poem's last line. During a vacation in the mountains, I was returning to our room by way of a shortcut behind the restaurant where we had breakfasted. There wasn't even a path where I walked, and within ten feet there was a sharp drop-off into a deep gorge. Suddenly I froze. Not two feet ahead of me was a snake. As we looked each other over, I held my breath and wondered what I should do. After a moment, however, the snake slithered on toward the restaurant as if he too wanted to eat his breakfast. Immediately I thought of the last lines of Dickinson's poem about a snake (the "narrow fellow"):

> Yet never met this fellow,
> Attended or alone,
> Without a tighter breathing,
> And zero at the bone.*

Since that day I can explain why those words "zero" and "bone" are exactly right. Interestingly, there's much about that poem that still strikes me as mediocre, but the last line is an honest dramatization of man face to face with nature.

When we teach by sharing a personal experience like that, we assume that all students will be drawn to the subject as we were. But suppose some of my students weren't afraid of snakes. They

---

*Emily Dickinson, *Complete Poems*, ed. Thomas H. Johnson (Boston: Little, Brown, 1960), p. 460.

might want to know what kind I had seen. If I confessed it was only a garden snake, they would probably conclude that both Dickinson and I were cravens. Other students may remain unmoved because something of one's excitement is always lost in the telling. When we introduce a subject, we frequently don't make converts right away, and, after all, I had taught that poem many times before liking it very much myself.

Persons outside the teaching profession often wonder how teachers can remain enthusiastic about presenting the same subject year in and year out. How can a science teacher who's been explaining for fifteen years how the heart works be very eager to go over the process a sixteenth time? Fortunately, the very act of leading a class generates a certain amount of excitement in most teachers, and new students may always ask slightly different questions. No one, though, can pretend that excitement about any given idea does not diminish over a period of time. What a teacher does is to try to convey his original enthusiasm for an idea. If the science teacher was excited the first time he truly understood the details of the heartbeat, there's a good chance he can inspire students about that too. Their interest, in turn, may rekindle the teacher's own eagerness.

To entice students to engage in a new activity, a teacher usually has to do more than verbally describe it. Frequently he must force students to become at least passive participants in the new experience by listening or watching. Therefore, a teacher who is also a skilled performer is more successful. Students may be intrigued by watching a calculus teacher solve a difficult equation, a PE teacher drive a ball 250 yards down the fairway, a typing teacher click away at 90 words a minute, or an English teacher recite Hamlet's soliloquy. I once heard a student complain that in three years at a conservatory he never heard most of his instructors perform at all. That suggested to him either that they couldn't play very well or that they didn't care enough about their students to want to play for them. He felt he would have been more attracted to difficult new pieces had he heard his teachers play them before they were assigned.

As students become interested in a new activity, they need free rein to explore it. A teacher should take their comments and questions seriously; many side issues can be explored with good results. One day a student of mine was presenting to the class a story he had written about surfing. I was so proud of him because while his narrative was short, it was a poignant coming-of-age tale. As we began our discussion, one of his classmates asked why the main character had to wax his surfboard. I didn't openly express my disappointment, but I thought any nincompoop should see that the story was not about wax but about a young boy's attempt to understand his relationship to physical nature. Happily that day I was not leading the discussion. The writer of the story knew all about waxes; he also knew that most of his classmates skied instead of surfed, so he compared waxing surfboards with waxing cross-country skiis. His intuition was exactly right. The question had seemed simplistic and tangential to me, but because it was answered knowledgeably it led to questions about other details of surfing.

A beginner in any subject has at least one advantage over a more informed person. Because everything about the subject is new to the beginner, he can feel like a discoverer. He senses the wonder that a toddler does coming upon the first daffodil of spring. The child doesn't know that anybody before him has ever seen such a flower. He proudly exhibits it to his parents as his find. Suppose instead of rejoicing with him, a parent said, "Well, yes, it is pretty, but daffodils come up every spring." Teachers are often guilty of a variation of that response. A student comes to his teacher excitedly with what he thinks is a new insight about the subject. Besides admitting that he's pleased the student is using his head, the teacher will almost always add, "Of course, the idea was published a number of years ago." There are numerous ways for a teacher to impress students that he is an expert on his subject, but that is not one of them.

To do the opposite, one teacher even went so far as to allow a student to spend several weeks building a gadget he hoped to market but one that the teacher knew had already been manufactured. If that seems heartless, what was the teacher's alternative? How would the student have felt had his teacher told him not to bother with his invention? He would have thought there was nothing he could contribute to the field, an impression that would have been entirely false. His idea was no less significant because someone else thought of it first. If he must learn, as this student eventually did, that he was not first, it is better to derive that from a neutral source, such as a catalogue of various devices, than from the belief that his ideas were unworthy in his teacher's eyes.

I remember how defeated I felt once when a professor of mine assigned our class a term paper on John Milton. He sent us out to the library for who knows how many hours of research with these concluding remarks: "There is nothing you can discover about Milton that has not previously been published. Don't try to be creative; just analyze what others have said." By the time he gave that advice, he had probably been grading Milton papers for forty years; he must have been sick of them. He realized that with our limited resources and our inexperience, the chances of our coming upon a new fact or idea were unlikely. But discoveries are always unlikely. Students can and do make them as well as anybody else. He had no right to deceive us and he also had no right to dampen—nay, drown—our enthusiasm.

To further students' enthusiasm, a teacher must convince them that whatever task they undertake is important for them to do. Moreover, they should feel that their teacher has confidence they can do it and that he will help them overcome their difficulties. Naturally, a teacher shouldn't say or imply to a student that he has the ability of an Einstein if the teacher is wondering how the student is going to pass ninth-grade science. However, if that same student himself dreams of becoming a theoretical physicist, does he actually gain anything by direct discouragement from his teacher? Of course, this does not suggest that a teacher should not acquaint him with some specific difficulties of the task and hence help him to judge his ability objectively.

Finally, even though an expanded range of interests is usually an advantage, it is not always an unmixed blessing. Because of the development of different interests, an individual may become isolated from the very people he has been closest to. The point was dramatized on a television broadcast about an Indian scientist in the Southwest. Going to college and graduate school allowed him to answer many of the questions about the universe he had pondered as a boy on the reservation. He also began to appreciate much more of history, literature, and music. At the same time he lost ties with his family. To be sure, he still felt compelled to visit his tribe from time to time, but he visited as a stranger. Many people undergo this man's dilemma, if to a less startling degree. Ironically, by the time a person begins to realize that he has become different from those in his early environment, it is usually too late for him to retreat. And few would actually wish to, even though they may also regret what they leave behind.

Goal 3: Self-discipline

Without deference to friends or family, each person should be able to decide what kind of life he wishes to lead. To stick by his choices, he must have self-discipline. Notwithstanding, self-discipline is a concept frequently misunderstood. The multiple meanings for the word *discipline* probably account for some of this misinterpretation. Some imagine that a self-disciplined life is a life without pleasure. They believe that a self-disciplined person more or less inflicts punishment on himself by constantly striving for improvement. He would never watch a thriller if he could be seeing a nature program instead. Others, who champion the trait, make exaggerated claims for it, including the one often heard in schools that there is no learning without self-discipline. This belief suggests that a person must have self-discipline *before* he begins to learn, whereas in reality the concentration requisite for learning fosters the development of this trait. A child may have very little self-discipline when he learns to eat peas with his fork without spilling them; the fact that he learns to do this, though, means that he has acquired more control over his actions than he had when he ate with his spoon or with his hand. By extension, a person who is highly self-disciplined is able to control more and more of what he does. This does not mean, by the way, that he makes unattainable demands on himself. He knows that he can't become a professional dancer merely because he practices eight hours a day.

Self-discipline is essential for successful achievement in most skills. Does anyone imagine that a person who wants to perfect the performance of a task works at it day after day simply because he enjoys it? He does it because he understands this is the only way he can improve. The moments of breakthrough never come if all he does is wait for them. He must force them, often plodding with great uncertainty. When he least expects it, something clicks, he gets an insight, and he's able to improve. Small wonder, then, that such control increases self-esteem, which, in turn, feeds future success.

Any discipline imposed on a student in school is to increase his self-discipline. A certain amount of self-discipline is exacted merely by requiring attendance in classes. Demanding orderly behavior takes students one step further, and requiring them to work in class and to prepare homework, still further. Naturally, students are going to resist some of the discipline meted out. Like the boy in the introductory example in this chapter, many of my students complain vociferously about having to conform precisely to instructions about length of compositions. They don't realize that much skill is required to express content within a specified number of words. They also argue that as long as they complete an assignment, submitting it on Wednesday instead of Tuesday should not matter. The question is, though, whether many of them would have the work ready even by Wednesday had it not been prescribed for Tuesday. A person who is highly self-disciplined doesn't need others to establish deadlines for him. If one is indicated, he usually completes the task by the time it's called for. Most of us, however, lack that kind of control. Having a deadline actually helps us get to the work, and of course no deadline is meaningful unless a penalty exists for ignoring it.

If a teacher has a legitimate rationale for his procedures, it need not concern him unduly that students fail to grasp that purpose. When I was in college, one of my history professors tried to instill habits of careful research in us. Most of us, though, simply thought he was a stickler because he required us to take and submit notes that were mostly paraphrased and that were written on one side of a three-by-five card. Because we thought he was treating us like fifth-graders, some of us openly rebelled and refused to show him our notes. I passed that course, as well as many others, before I realized the value of what he was trying to teach us. As he said (and as I try to teach my students too), a research paper is largely written at the time one finishes his investigation, provided he has made careful notes, because he cannot make careful notes unless he has truly thought about the subject. The paper is also easily organized. Many of my students, however, are just as skeptical as I was.

A disciplined person has developed separate procedures for most activities. Isn't this why we can do something like dressing ourselves with little thought and with great haste if we wish? Each of us has a routine, a set sequence of steps, for putting on a given item of clothing. We take that routine entirely for granted unless an accident or illness incapacitates us and forces us to master a new sequence. The fact that the procedure for each of us is somewhat unique explains why we frequently feel awkward if somebody assists us in putting on a garment. Nobody else does it exactly as we would. Many of our activities are just that routine. Why is it, for example, that when we write a report we can concentrate solely on its content rather than on the physical act of writing? That happens because each of us has a certain way to form each letter. If a person starts a small *a* at midway its eventual height, he'll do that every time he writes an *a*, just as another person might invariably begin his *a*'s closer to their peak. Where a letter is begun, the result of early education, is not so important as the definite procedure for starting and completing the letter. Once a child is secure with a method of forming a letter, he doesn't even have to look to write.

Routines are also essential for the most creative of activities, the romantic notion about routines stifling creativity notwithstanding. A prima ballerina's movements appear effortless because in the beginning of her training her feet were placed, sometimes repeatedly, in a given position. She was then required to hold that stance until it became second nature to her. Similarly, when a concert pianist learns a selection, he learns to strike each note of the piece with a certain finger; if he varies that fingering, he makes a mistake. He doesn't have time, though, while he's in concert to think that he wants to strike, say middle C with his thumb one time and with his third finger the next. The interesting point is that he doesn't have to think about it. Once he's truly learned a piece, all he has to do is start it. Subsequent notes come as automatically to him as our forming of letters does after we have learned to write. This is why people are advised to learn manual skills so that they can be performed with the least effort; relearning is extremely difficult.

Artists develop other kinds of routines as well. Many even set aside the same hours of each day for work, a technique to ensure they'll get started. They also develop routines within this framework. For example, Hemingway, who always worked in the mornings, liked to spend the first part of each session revising what he had written the previous day. Some writers like to conclude their stints only when their work is going well; others prefer to revise at the end of each day. The important point is that each person develops a habitual procedure for himself. Then he doesn't feel right unless he sticks to it.

Nevertheless, students are apt to reject the idea of a routine because that word is closely linked in many minds with boredom. We feel sorry for factory workers because they have to do exactly the same thing each day. However, if we examine the matter thoughtfully, we realize that the routine itself is not the problem. A man who makes bracelets by hand has a procedure for that task just as well as a man who works in a jewelry factory. The reason the factory worker's routine bores him while the craftsman's doesn't is that the craftsman sets his own pace and he, rather than a machine, fashions the finished product. While the routine of the assembly line may enslave a worker, that of the craftsman's actually frees him to work more creatively. Like the craftsman, we all soon find that we are more productive if we have a variety of routines we can take for granted to help us accomplish what we wish. This is not to say, though, that some days we shouldn't just go to the park.

Goal 4: Good Judgment

Good judgment, another characteristic of a successful life, rests on rationality. The trouble is, though, that none of us is or probably wishes to be totally rational all of the time. Were we so, there would be no billion-dollar advertising industry. Sometimes a person seems less human by allowing his reason to predominate over his emotion. Imagine an ice fishing party of two fathers with their two young sons. The boys wander away from their fathers onto thin ice. It breaks and they are submerged. As they begin screaming, both fathers run instinctively in the direction of their cries. One father, however, is much more cautious than the other. He sees the problem and goes back to their station to fetch a rope. The other inches forward, disregarding danger to himself. He is able to touch their fingers before he, along with the boys, is engulfed by the frigid waters. If he dies because of his attempt, we would not count him a foolish man. We would probably say that he *sacrificed* his life for his son.

When we're strictly honest, though, we realize that much of what we call bad luck is actually poor judgment. In this simple example the father's attempted rescue was noble, but it wouldn't have been necessary had he exercised better common sense. The children should never have been allowed to stray to unsafe ice in the first place. Sometimes we act imprudently because we fail to think through a situation. At other times we play the odds, so to speak. We disregard information, trusting that we can escape without calamity. The following, less catastrophic example also illustrates the idea. On arriving at his house during a snowstorm, a man parked his car on the street in order to shovel his driveway before putting his car in the garage. Even in good weather he didn't like to leave his car at the curb, but he reasoned that the snow would be more easily removed if it were not packed down by the weight of the car. While it occurred to him that drivers frequently lose control of their vehicles during storms, he rationalized that he needed only ten minutes to clear his drive. How did he feel, though, when two minutes before he would have completed the job he looked up to see another car skidding into his?

Wishful thinking also interferes with sound judgment. Con men very reasonably and regularly set their traps for anyone gullible enough to fall for the ploy that he can have something for nothing. And who isn't attracted by that idea? Usually time is a factor in these gimmicks: if a person doesn't act today, the chance won't be his tomorrow.

One of the curses of an age of specialization such as ours is that we are often forced to decide a matter without sufficient information. We can be taken advantage of anywhere from hospitals to car shops. Notwithstanding, our temptation usually is to laugh at anyone who lets himself be duped, no matter whom or what he may be able to blame. People are expected to know how the world works and how best to survive in it. Such practical judgment begins with acquiring information and then relating that prudently to new situations. It is a trait that requires nurturing. Suppose a small child munches green apples until his stomach aches. Does he learn from that experience to eschew green apples or to avoid eating large quantities of them? His logic might well lead him to renounce apples altogether unless those around him help him to interpret his predicament and hence lead him to a more thoughtful decision.

However much we may need guidance like that as we grow, it too can become an obstacle to good judgment. Eventually each person should stand alone. He should base his decisions on what his own reason tells him is true, no matter how authoritative voices urging the contrary might seem. Those voices are varied and many: "Why won't you study to be a doctor? I'm your mother and I want only what's best for you." . . . "Do people seem to avoid you? Perhaps it's time you considered a mouthwash." . . . "Why don't you like this sculpture? Anyone with discerning taste will observe at once its obvious superiority." Home, church, school, government, specialists of all sorts, advertisers—they all seem to conspire against us at times. The extent to which a person can resist them depends as much on the information he acquires as it does on his own character.

When I was little I was taught in Sunday school that the Greeks were barbarians because they were polytheistic. (My teacher didn't use that word.) Later, when my college professors spoke of the contributions of the Greeks to Western civilization, I was quite bewildered at first. It took me a long time to understand why I was so unreceptive to that idea; I couldn't believe that my Sunday school teacher had influenced me to think in a wrong direction.

Another incident involved an acquaintance of mine who had purchased a new painting. As I visited his home one day, he proudly pointed to the work displayed conspicuously over his mantel. He mentioned that while I may not have heard of this painter before, I soon would be hearing a great deal. He added that "someone who knew what he was talking about" had told him that this artist's ideas were "daring and innovative." His particular painting, he had been assured, would soon be worth many times what he had paid for it. When I asked him if he himself enjoyed the painting, he admitted that he didn't. Then he asked, "What does my opinion about a painting matter?" I was stunned. I can understand buying almost anything that promises good return on an investment, but didn't he have someplace to store that work besides over his fireplace?

A third example of uncritical submission to authority involved a graduate student at a respected university. He allowed himself to be cowed by a book. This student informed one of his professors that an explanation in his previous lecture was incorrect. When the teacher asked why, the student replied that the textbook presented an opposing idea. From the student's point of view, it was impossible for a person to know more than a book. That story may seem shocking because we feel that such an advanced student should have known better, but most of us place inordinate faith in the printed page. Isn't this why we often hear others say (or perhaps say ourselves), "Yes, but this must be true. I read it somewhere." The ability of print to convince seems downright astounding, given the various ways errors creep into texts. Sometimes there are out-and-out attempts to deceive. At other times there may be so-called honest mistakes; these, nevertheless, are errors, resulting often from insufficient research. In addition, printing mistakes frequently abound. Notwithstanding, much unfamiliar information appears plausible in print. If we think we should know something that we don't, the print can literally overwhelm our judgment.

Few adults escape the intimidation of authority altogether, no matter how lofty their university degrees. For teen-agers just beginning to assert independence, the matter is especially treacherous. They are often tempted to reject authority merely because it is that. Suppose a father advises his son to wear a clean shirt and tie when he goes for a job interview. The son reasons, "What does he know? He thinks that because he had to wear a tie in his day, I do too. Anyway, he can't tell me what to do anymore." His father's opinion may or may not be correct, but the fact that it is his father's should not count. What the young man needs to consider is what kind of attire is likely to land him the job.

There is nothing inherently good about independent judgment. Its value lies in freeing us from harmful outside influences. Sometimes it's good judgment to seek outside help. Imagine that I had ten thousand dollars to invest in stocks. If I pretended with my limited financial expertise that I knew as much as an experienced broker about which stocks would yield the best returns, I would probably soon lose my capital. In a classroom, the teacher is the expert on his subject.

Students frequently think that independence of judgment is not truly encouraged in classrooms. This is why they often ask in the beginning of a course whether they are free to disagree with what the teacher says about the subject. While the answer to that ought to be apparent to anybody, the issue is complicated. Many times students think they have simply challenged a teacher's opinion on the subject matter, when in actuality they have also challenged the teacher's authority to maintain order. Suppose a student objects to a teacher's interpretation of a given point. The student gives his reasons for a different view, but his teacher finds logical flaws in each of his ideas. Even though the student can't think of any way to counter his teacher's objections, he sulks. To get even, he talks to a friend or reads a book or does something else he's not supposed to do while the lesson is continued. If he persists with this misbehavior long enough to be corrected, he will almost inevitably feel that he has been unjustly reprimanded for disagreeing with his teacher. At this time nothing can be said to convince the student otherwise.

In trying to help his students see that one opinion is not necessarily as good as another, a teacher often appears dogmatic to them. This is especially true in courses like history and literature, because words are subject to interpretation. A given word, though, cannot mean anything we wish it to. As an example, students often argue against my assertion that Huckleberry Finn is prejudiced. Prejudice to them is so contemptible that anyone as loving and kind and good as Huck cannot possibly be prejudiced. If they leave the novel thinking that Huck is altogether wonderful, they have ignored countless dramatic instances in that book establishing his prejudice. More importantly, if they are allowed to misinterpret the book, they will be oblivious to instances of prejudice in their own lives because they do not understand what that word means. The point I want my students to grasp, though, is not that my opinion is better than theirs because it is mine but because in this case my reasons are sounder than theirs.

This lesson is usually more palatable to them if they do not feel that their personal opinions or those of the teacher are at stake. For this reason assigning an analysis of contrasting views of one and the same historical or literary person or event is often effective. Assume an American history class is considering the character and contributions of the Puritans to American society. Students can enjoy discussing whether the seventeenth-century account of William Bradford or that of Thomas Morton is more convincing in explaining why the Puritans cut down their neighbors' Maypole at Merrymount, Massachusetts. Even though the students are formulating their opinions about Bradford's and Morton's ideas, the discussion can focus on the reasons of the two authors rather than on the students' opinions. Such an assignment is exciting, too, because it allows students to glimpse how history books are written.

Regardless of their boldness in the humanities, students are usually more hesitant about challenging math and science topics. They believe that in those courses they are learning facts rather than currently accepted ideas. That those opinions may change in time the teacher knows very well, but he cannot spend the day qualifying. Even when a student thinks that he sees a fault with current thinking, his teacher's responsibility is to urge caution. Those ideas did not come about in a day. A student who expects to disprove them shouldn't be in a hurry either. Suppose a science student questions his teacher's lesson on pain. The teacher asserts that pain originates in nerve impulses throughout the body. If this is true, the student wonders, why did his grandmother no longer suffer pain in her leg after she had a brain operation? The teacher says that the brain must interpret the message of the nerve in order for pain to be felt, and he also tries to convince the student why it seems obvious that pain must start in the place of injury. A person's very eyes tell him that he has pricked his finger, not his brain. Still the student is dissatisfied; it doesn't seem a closed case to him. He reasons that if we feel no pain when a part of our brain is removed or destroyed, then we must experience our brains, not our external environment.

Though such a boy may have the makings of a scientist, his immediate dilemma may center around what answer he should write on the test of that subject. On a multiple-choice exam, he'll have to select "nerve impulses" as the correct answer if he expects credit. That doesn't imply that the test is poor or that the teacher hasn't allowed him to challenge authority. If the student should ever attempt to substantiate his own theory, it will be important for him to know how others regard pain. He may feel better if he has a chance to write not only what others think about the matter but also to develop his reasons for a different opinion, but it's well for him to learn how to succeed at many different kinds of tests.

When students do poorly on an evaluation, many attempt to

manipulate a teacher's sympathy by implying that the test was too long or that personal complications prevented their doing their best work. One of my teachers dismissed such pleas by telling us in advance of the first exam that he realized most of our answers would be improved were we given a longer time to work. He, though, had to judge what we could do in a limited time. If we were insufficiently prepared, that would probably be reflected in our grades. (He pointed out too that insufficient preparation often causes students to think a test is longer than it should be.) If we misinterpreted a question, our grades would suffer, even though we might have known the correct answer. If we devoted too much time to one part of a test, we would be penalized. An exam was to test not only a student's information but also his good judgment about how to work properly under a test situation. That teacher believed that if he didn't help us with the latter, he wasn't properly preparing us for various evaluations we would face later in life.

Frequently individuals have to be allowed to make mistakes in order to improve their judgment. To have to witness faltering, though, goes against the grain of many well-intentioned teachers. They're likely to rush in at the first sign of anything amiss, volunteering, "Here, let me show you how to do that." All the person having trouble learns from the demonstration is that his instructor or helper can do something better than he. I was struck by how much our beginning zoology professor in college allowed us to err. He told us that when we severed the skin of our frog's back we should not injure muscles and nerves lying just below the surface. He then demonstrated how we were to hold the scalpel and the skin to make proper incisions. Extreme care was necessary, he warned, because we would only receive one frog during the entire semester. Most of us in that class, I imagine, had never before cut any flesh other than meat on our plates. The girl next to me was the first at our table to plunge; that's exactly what she did too, ruining much of the tissue for the laboratories of the following two weeks. It was unnecessary for her to show the professor what she had done; he had watched her. When she complained that it was unfair for her to be penalized so much for a first mistake, he merely pointed out that he had no more frogs.

That same man taught us to read labels on containers before we used their contents. Just because a liquid is pink, he reminded us, doesn't necessarily mean the substance is what we think it is. He told us a story about someone he knew who had rushed to his medicine cabinet seeking relief for abdominal cramps. Several moments later that person was gagging; he had swallowed a mouthful of pink skin lotion instead of Pepto-Bismol. As impersonal as that teacher seemed to us then, though, I don't think he would have knowingly allowed us to hurt ourselves irreparably. A student who loses his eyes in an explosion because he hasn't read labels will certainly deplore his lack of judgment. However, if his teacher could have prevented the explosion, he is guilty of worse judgment than his student.

I recall a particular senior who suffered greatly because he lacked good judgment. He was at a total loss as to how long it would take him to do something, a difficulty exacerbated by his perfectionism. Frequently he came to me weeping because he was unable to accomplish what he thought he should. In addition to trying to help this boy set up a study schedule for himself, I found myself as a teacher in the extremely unusual position of counseling against perfection. He had been taught, as I was, always to do his best, but he hadn't truly considered what that involves. There are times when perfection is not only unexpected but also useless. If a person is applying two coats of paint to a wall, the first coat need not be free of brushmarks; the same principle holds if one is asked to submit a rough draft of an essay. A shrewd student learns to judge the intent of an assignment, as well as the amount of time he can afford to devote to the work. He doesn't spend, as this boy did, several days polishing a short rough draft, in the meantime neglecting altogether his other subjects. The boy thought that learning the information of subjects was all that was important in school; he didn't understand that school was also to help him develop habits and characteristics that would benefit him long after a good portion of the information was forgotten.

Sometimes good judgment involves moral issues. Naturally the same choice will not appear best to everybody. One person may be able to justify not reporting all of his income on his tax return, while another thinks that the lawlessness of that action would invite chaos. We are all guided in these matters by our philosophical and religious beliefs. No matter how strong their personal convictions, teachers should not try to legislate morality. Parents have legitimate grounds for objecting to teachers' attempting to influence their youngsters morally unless they are enrolled in a religious school. Say a teacher is a pacifist and tries to instill that value in his students. That would seem as inappropriate to anyone with opposing views as trying to influence students to be jingoistic would appear to a pacifist. An approach like that is not a teacher's prerogative.

At the same time, a teacher may influence students' beliefs even without wanting or trying to. Students seek teachers' advice on ethical decisions from time to time. If their questions are sincere, there's usually no reason to avoid answering them directly. What a student like this actually wants is to be relieved of the decision. A teacher probably helps him best by refusing to assume the responsibility and pointing out various ways he can view his problem.

In education the end result is what matters. After completing a program of instruction, will a person have attained a higher level of education? Many times educators are sidetracked into thinking that matters like happiness and self-fulfillment should be taught in high school. Although these states of mind may be incidental by-products of education, one should realize that they cannot be taught. Objectives like good family relationships and good citizenship, frequently introduced goals of high school education, can be expounded to a certain extent, but the question is whether they should be. Perhaps a more subtle confusion arises from discussions of various types of curricula. Some have urged a curriculum fostering creativity. Students should be required not merely to learn what others have done but also to use their own minds to write, paint, and invent. Others hold that students should learn useful subjects. They should graduate knowing how to earn a living. These issues require clarification.

First of all, an education cannot make anyone smart or creative. While those characteristics can unfortunately be stifled in schools, they cannot be demanded unless students happen to possess the qualities innately. Many very intelligent and creative persons have little education, and conversely it is possible to have a considerable degree of information without being particularly intelligent or imaginative. Therefore, in a school composed of average youngsters, a curriculum featuring a course in the history of painting is sounder than one with instruction in painting, although ideally both selections should be offered. Anyone appreciates a skill more if he has at least some personal knowledge of how it is performed. Beyond an elementary level, anyone wishing to develop a skill must have training in that area.

The terms "training" and "education" are often used interchangeably. There is a difference, though, shown by the fact that the same subject is training for one person and education for another. To most persons the study of history is education, but to a future historian that study constitutes his training. Strictly defined, training is preparation for a given trade or profession. Because the word has never carried the prestige that "education" does, training is usually associated with lines of work such as stenography or auto mechanics, which supposedly do not require a long time to master. If we're talking about a nurse's preparation, for instance, we say training, but if we're referring to a doctor's study, we normally say medical education. A doctor's preparation is training just as much as a nurse's, albeit of a more sophisticated nature. They are both learning how to earn their living.

The aim of education is to enrich life, but not in a monetary sense. Failure to understand this has resulted not only in confusion about what subjects should properly be taught in high schools and colleges but also in confusion in some Americans' minds about the very value of education. Many were outraged a few years ago when they realized that for the first time in our history having a college degree did not necessarily guarantee one a better job than he could have without it. As a car mechanic pointed out to me, what good was his wife's master's degree if she made less money than he and he had only a year's post-high school work with GM?

Fewer people would be tempted to denigrate education in this way had they been exposed to a rigorous one, no matter at what level. Too often, though, the assumption behind curriculum planning in high school is that courses of substance should be saved for youngsters going to college. The reasoning is that anyone who wants to be something like an auto mechanic would be uninterested in science or literature or philosophy. One trouble with such thinking is that too often it leads mainly to babysitting, and when this happens, the mechanic will reject the value of his education. While he may not need liberal arts courses for his work, he will need them to lead a full life. Actually, the fewer years one devotes to schooling, the more important it is that those years be used effectively.

Parents and teachers often speak of *giving* children an education as the most precious gift. However, since education is the interaction of information and character, it is not something to be given but rather something to be attained. Everybody achieves a certain degree of education, whether or not he goes to school. No one is ever as educated as he might be. If students have successfully begun their ascent of this scale by the time they graduate from high school, teachers can be pleased.

VII
Rewards of Teaching

Imagine a discussion in which so many hands are raised that the teacher doesn't know whom to call on first. Students are excited about the subject; they don't wait to be recognized before volunteering their points of view. The ensuing debate might even be called an argument. The teacher doesn't have to do anything; he just stands back and listens to students take the subject apart.

Classes like this sometimes occur.

Imagine next a discussion in which nobody says anything. The teacher asks a question only to find that after unsuccessfully trying to coax the answer from several students, he must answer it himself. Some heads go down on desks; others stare into space. The teacher begins to feel nervous; he's been taught that a good teacher should be able to make any class interesting. The harder he works, though, the thicker grows the wall between him and the students. Eventually he feels he's talking totally to himself.

Classes like this also occur.

Of course, if all classes were like the first, the rewards of teaching would not require enumeration. The knowledge that one can do a job well is probably the most important compensation any worker can have. However, even though stark extremes like the above are more typical for most teachers at the beginning of their careers, success in teaching cannot be continuous. First, a teacher's success is not dependent solely upon himself. Moreover, the way an individual measures his own achievement is in part determined by his character. No matter how much others may esteem his ability, a person who is highly self-critical and who understands the magnitude of a task like teaching will seldom feel as successful as someone with lower standards and lesser understanding.

Truthfully, there are days any teacher feels that his is a thankless task. A friend of mine who has taught for many years quipped that it would be a mark of my courage if I left a blank page under the heading "rewards." I know that I leave school many days thinking that scrubbing floors or washing dishes would be more satisfying than teaching because at least in those jobs one could see what he had accomplished. Also, students are frequently rebellious or cantankerous; they don't want a teacher to do for them what he's trying to do, at least not at the time he's doing it. The frustration caused a teacher by such an attitude is captured precisely in John Updike's story "Home." One of the characters remarks that even though his father had been a public school teacher for thirty years, he still "believed in education."[*]

As honest as these bleak representations may be, they are but one part of the canvas. When teachers get no other remuneration, there's always payday. If money is one's sole motivation, however, teaching is a poor choice of work. The highest salary teachers can hope for provides only modest support even for a small family. Last year I was talking with a senior who had started to drive trucks for his living. Upon his graduation, he expected to make as much money as I do after more than a decade of teaching. Teachers do, though, have a measure of job security missing from many other lines of work. While individual teachers may find their positions terminated, most schools remain open even in periods of severe economic depression. And

---

[*]In *Pigeon Feathers and Other Stories* (Greenwich, Conn.: Fawcett Premier, 1962), p. 108.

a good omen that the tangible benefits of teaching may increase in years to come is that most teachers no longer think it is unprofessional to demand such improvements. Workers are seldom paid very much unless they constantly compare their own efforts with those of others and insist on being compensated on an equal basis.

Often people who don't teach like to complain about the "soft" life teachers lead. They point out that high school teachers always have their free periods and that the school day itself is over in the middle of the afternoon. (That no teacher ever completes his work entirely during the school hours does not seem to occur to them.) They also cite numerous vacations as evidence that a teacher doesn't work very much. They enjoy suggesting that a teacher looks forward to those vacations as much as students do.

In the old days lengthy vacations were built into the school year primarily because youngsters had to work at home. Though the periods off have been greatly reduced today, they remain in school calendars because students and teachers need them. Learning requires concentration and routine seldom demanded in other work, but a variety of routine is also essential if the concentration is to be effectively sustained. As a teacher I am willing to work at nights and on weekends, as I must, but I would think twice about giving that much overtime if I did not have my vacations to look forward to. Moreover, teaching is not the kind of work that can be put down and forgotten. A week must often elapse before a teacher can feel that he's gotten away from it at all. Why am I justifying? I personally would despise working at any job fifty weeks a year, although I realize that many people do. The days leading up to a vacation are inevitably exhilarating. There's a sense of an endless stretch of time ahead even though the holiday may be one of only several days. If schools eventually must be in session the year round, as some fear economics will dictate, I hope my own career will have ended by then. Teaching could never be the same without our vacations!

Most teachers are also attracted to their work because of the independence it affords. When they walk into their classrooms, they are in charge. Nobody tells them what to do and how to do it. Naturally they have supervisors, but good supervisors don't try to boss teachers. To a certain extent teachers can decide what topics of their subjects they want to teach, as well as how to teach them.

It cannot be said that teaching entails no pressure, but much of the pressure a teacher puts upon himself. While there is more and more talk of accountability in teaching, it will always be a "many mistakes" job. Like students, teachers also learn from mistakes. If a teacher had to fear losing his job the first or second time he erred, the kind of threat under which many people work, he would never be able to become a good teacher. The peculiar thing is that often no one else is even aware of a teacher's blunders unless he broadcasts them himself.

Some people are going to exert themselves more than others in any profession. It's easy, though, to get by with being a lazy teacher, and, paradoxically, a lazy teacher is not necessarily a bad one. A teacher's freedom to determine the amount of effort he will invest in his work is captured in a little story that few besides teachers can truly appreciate. One thinks of any obscure work by someone who is well known, be he poet, musician, historian, or scientist. Then a conversation between two teachers is constructed. The first teacher asks the second whether he's read, say, Shakespeare's *Timon of Athens*. The second responds, "Read it? I haven't even taught it yet." The first teacher bursts into laughter.

On the other hand, anyone who thrives on work will not find a profession more to his liking than teaching. A teacher has the bonus, too, of feeling that his is work useful to others as well as to himself. Just to continue learning one's own subject is work enough for a lifetime—and reward enough too. It's one thing to know material well enough to pass a college course; it's quite another to know that same material sufficiently to teach it well. A teacher has to be able to answer questions that perhaps he's never anticipated, and that while he's before a class. He has to be able to explain complex matters simply. Such rediscovery of one's subject is strenuous work, but it's also one of the reasons a person can enjoy teaching the same subject repeatedly.

Imagine how many jobs there are in which an individual must feel that a machine could do his work as well as if not better than he. Machines can certainly be used to good effect in instruction, but they will never replace teachers. A machine can't answer the student's spur-of-the-moment question; a machine can't insist that a student do his work; a machine can't encourage him. As long as people lack the self-discipline to educate themselves, which has been the case with the great majority of people throughout history, they will need teachers.

When people reminisce about their school days, they think of individual teachers more often than they do about subjects they studied. "Remember Miss So-and-So with those toothpick legs?" . . . "Remember old So-and-So? The minute he personally wasn't talking for five minutes, he'd nod off." . . . "What was that teacher's name? Remember the day he let fire at Bill with his ruler?" . . . "Oh yes, Miss So-and-So. She worked our fingers to the bones." Even though much of their banter is somewhat mocking, there's usually also a note of affection in it. In fact, most high school students seem to like most of their teachers. Students may enjoy having a substitute for a day or two—they understand that's a day off for them—but they usually don't like having their regular teacher out for an extended period. When one of my colleagues had a gall bladder operation, his students wrote him a get-well card saying that he had some "gall" to leave them. Of course they couldn't resist the pun, but I know from talking to those youngsters that there was a sense in which they felt deserted. Their class wasn't the same without their regular teacher. It happens that I teach some students for both their junior and senior years. When I told those juniors last year that I would be away from school during this one, they were sincerely disappointed. Even though I knew that my replacement was excellent, I was pleased that it mattered to them that I would not be their teacher.

The phrase "molding young minds" makes me think of mildew or sculpturing, but we often do influence students, whether or not we set out directly to do so. I used to think that a person's character was already determined by the time he reached high school, so the difference an individual teacher could make on any student would be minimal. The first year I taught, though, a thoughtful student made me wonder if I had been right about that. "Do you really think teachers don't influence us?" he asked. That seems to be just the point too: we affect rather than determine students' characters. Even so, in no single instance can I spell out the exact manner in which I have influenced them; I also know that my character speaks more than my words. Finally, though, manner and extent don't matter. If students feel I have helped them, that's a tremendous rewrd for me.

The supreme example of teacher influence was probably that of Socrates on Plato. Everybody's heard of Socrates, but no one would have had not his pupil Plato devoted a good part of his life to writing about his teacher's character, deeds, and philosophy. Most of us don't hope for that kind of influence. Numerous stories, however, impress upon me that teaching is a profession in which the individual can feel that he makes a difference. My mother before me was a high school English teacher. At her funeral I was introduced to a man whom she had taught some fifty years earlier. One of my brothers later joked that her lessons hadn't rubbed off very much on that particular student because he couldn't even spell "dog." I wondered if my mother would have remembered that man who drove a considerable distance to be at his teacher's last rites. Whether she would have or not, though, his presence was testimony enough.

INDEX